MW00534221

The Mestizo/a Community of the Spirit

Princeton Theological Monograph Series

K. C. Hanson, Charles M. Collier, D. Christopher Spinks,
Series Editors

Recent volumes in the series:

Richard Valantasis et al., editors
The Subjective Eye: Essays in Honor of Margaret Miles

Anette Ejsing
A Theology of Anticipation: A Constructive Study of C. S. Peirce

Caryn Riswold
Coram Deo: Human Life in the Vision of God

Paul O. Ingram, editor
Constructing a Relational Cosmology

Michael G. Cartwright
*Practices, Politics, and Performance: Toward a Communal
Hermeneutic for Christian Ethics*

David A. Ackerman
*Lo, I Tell You a Mystery: Cross, Resurrection,
and Paraenesis in the Rhetoric of 1 Corinthians*

Lloyd Kim
*Polemic in the Book of Hebrews:
Anti-Judaism, Anti-Semitism, Supersessionism?*

The Mestizo/a Community of the Spirit

A Postmodern Latino/a Ecclesiology

OSCAR GARCÍA-JOHNSON

☙PICKWICK *Publications* · Eugene, Oregon

THE MESTIZO/A COMMUNITY OF THE SPIRIT
A Postmodern Latino/a Ecclesiology

Princeton Theological Monograph Series 105

Copyright © 2009 Oscar García-Johnson. All rights reserved. Except for brief quotations in critical articles or reviews, no part of this book may be reproduced in any manner without prior written permission from the publisher. Write: Permissions, Wipf and Stock Publishers, 199 W. 8th Ave., Suite 3, Eugene, OR 97401.

Unless otherwise stated, quotations from the Bible are taken from the *New Revised Standard Version,* © 1989, 1995 by the Division of Christian Education of The National Council of the Churches of the Christ of the United States of America.

ISBN 13: 978-1-55635-719-0

Cataloging-in-Publication data:

Oscar García-Johnson.

The mestizo/a community of the spirit : a postmodern latino/a ecclesiology / Oscar García-Johnson.

Princeton Theological Monograph Series 105

xviii + 156 p. ; 23 cm. —Includes bibliography

Eugene, Ore.: Pickwick Publications

ISBN 13: 978-1-55635-719-0

1. Liberation theology—United States. 2. Latin Americans—Religious life—United States. 3. Hispanic Americans—Religious life. I. Title. II. Series.

BT83.575 G1 2009

Manufactured in the U.S.A.

"Theologia a Deo docetur, Deum docet, et ad Deum ducit"
—Thomas Aquinas

To Margarita, my beloved mother,
who revealed God's cruciform love to me
To my wife, Karla who teaches me about God
To my son Chris, who leads me to God

Contents

Introduction

THE HISTORIC DEVELOPMENT AND CURRENT STATUS OF LATINO/A CUL-
ture in American life has revealed a path—has ascertained a religious
and sociocultural location—within the infrastructure of American society. Regardless of the conditions grounding Latinos/as in today's U.S.
territory, the fact is that Latinos/as are cultural citizens of the *always-
emerging* American culture (currently a population of over 44 million).
That fact alone should be sufficient, from a Christian perspective, to
justify and acknowledge the Latino/a *presence* in the theological academic establishment.

Life as experienced by Latino/a communities is a flux of realities
constantly shaping the social location, cultural consciousness, religious
life, political presence, and multicultural practices of these communities. In the same breath, the categories of understanding that so far have
been utilized in defining church life in the U.S. must be reconstructed
to reflect a more fluid and inclusive understanding of culture and the
church. Perhaps this work is an attempt to discern categories better able
to deal with Latino/a culture as heterogeneous as it is and the experiential realm of the Spirit of God in history. Although we have ventured to
undertake this task from *within* Latino/a theologizing, we believe this
project represents a challenge and a contribution to American theologizing and at large. So, we suggest considering our study as a journey,
pilgrimage or *commuting* of critical faith amid the most domestic *form*
of human territory, culture.

Motive and Aim

First a clarification, when referring to the *Latino/a church*, we do not
mean an adjectival categorization—that merely describes an "ethnic"
perception. If language is viewed as the preferred *hermeneutics* for
theological discourse then we are referring to a *grammatical* that is at

the same time a *substantival* category. Perhaps the concept of *gerunds* would apply better. Doing Latino/a ecclesiology means being part of the Latino/a culture and the eschatological Latino/a community—being Latino/a in the *present* and in the *becoming*. One cannot be church without being Latino/a, thus we are church *latinamente*; we are *mañana* (tomorrow) church.

We are convinced that Latino/a theologizing has a contribution to make to traditional theological discourses because of its methodology, cultural commitment, and practical spirituality. That fact and the ministry urgencies of the author for a Spirit-shaped and *transformational* cultural language able to permeate American's everyday life constitute the dominant motive for this work. The insisting question behind our theological reflections is *how can (Latino/a) theology function as theologia a Deo docetur, Deum docet, et ad Deum ducit* (theology taught by God, teaches of God, and leads to God).[1]

With this understanding in mind and acknowledging the fact that the Latino/a church is in practice a diverse, vigorous, and growing religious and cultural phenomenon in U.S. religious life, we envision our work as one contributing toward Christian ecclesiology by the elaboration of a *practical theology of the Spirit*. Such a theological paradigm, as we will see, is conceived as contemplating the life of the Latino/a church on a postmodern horizon. Our aim is that this theological paradigm will continue to be constructed and reconstructed to conform a critical apparatus for experience, reflection, and praxis.

We have ventured to call this paradigm *Latino/a (practical) theology of the Spirit* for three reasons. We call it *Latino/a* theology because it speaks *latinamente*, that is, in a way that does not dissociate Latino/a culture(s) from theological reflection. That said, we assume that the Latino/a theological voices that give content to our work fairly represent the practices, contexts, and hopes of the *always-emerging* Latino/a people of the U.S., however limited to our perception and interpretation.

We call it *practical* because it is Latino/a theology. As we will see, Latino/a theology uses a praxis-based methodology for grasping and understanding Latino/a forms of life, and proposing paradigms for ecclesial action.

1. This is a Thomistic definition of theology embraced by both Roman Catholics and Protestant (scholastics). See Muller, *Dictionary of Latin and Greek Theological Terms*, 299.

Finally, we call it *of the Spirit* because our paradigm recognizes the Holy Spirit—the Spirit of the resurrected Christ—to be (1) the author of Christian experience, (2) the shaping agent of communal life, and (3) the divine rhetorician who persuades and transform non-redeemed cultural geographies.

Latino/a theology of the Spirit shall be perceived as a crossroads theology, thus attention to *formative intersections* between God's Spirit and culture is of particular importance and constitutes the heuristics for theological reflection and production. In this particular work, our attention concentrates on the Latino/a church, understanding the same as the product of God's Spirit in *intersection* with Latino/a culture. Throughout our discussion, we will introduce the church as God's chosen cultural geography for authentic transformation of the culture and at large. The Latino/a missiologist Orlando Costas claimed, "Christ's transforming power is mediated by the work of the Spirit in the life and witness of the church. . . . The point, however, is not of theological precision and missiological awareness but, rather, of commitment and practice."[2]

We concur with Costas and suggest that authentic transformation is historically possible within a given cultural space and through a Christ-shaped cultural praxis or Christopraxis.

God is the author of the language of transformation; a rhetoric of love, joy, and hope which is to be embraced as the *presence of divine peace* in the *form* of human experience and cultural practices. Consequently, we venture to argue that Latino/a theology can transform Latino/a communities by becoming a (practical) *theology of the Spirit*—a critical discourse that *imagines* and *calls* the Latino/a church to conform to a *Mestizo/a Community of Mañana*. In this sense, *Latino/a theology of the Spirit* aims to align the church with its paradigmatic mission as *presence of divine peace*—the resurrected culture of Christ *in the world*—through a praxis that makes public its inclusive, communal, and eschatological character. The *Mestizo/a Community of Mañana* is the *Mestizo/a Community of the Spirit*, for the *Mañana* we refer to is God's imagined story brought about to the present by the Spirit of the resurrected Christ.

---

2. Costas, *Christ Outside the Gate*, 16.

Our work is in the direction of *painting* an image of the Christian community that *embodies* and *transmits* Latino/a renewed culture. The Spirit of God, evidently, is the central figure in making both Christian experience and community a concrete reality. The narratives of the Pentecost and the cross constitute the formative *juncture* informing our ecclesiological understanding of the church as a *cruciform community of the Spirit*. It is on this understanding that *Latino/a theology of the Spirit* is to be constructed.

We shall pursue this challenging pilgrimage through four chapters. Since we are proposing a further development within current Latino/a theologizing, we shall ask in our first chapter *In which way Latino/a theology is or not a practical theology?* We will produce a general survey on the matter of "practical theologies" hoping to identify Latino/a theology within those coordinates. We shall encounter an assorted variety of discourses in this arena out of which flourishes, in our view, Christopraxis and Latin American liberation theology. We will explore the particular influence of Latin American liberation theology on Latino/a theologizing encountering a methodological commonality. After a review of the Latino/a theological process, we shall conclude that Latino/a theology is essentially *a practical theology of culture*. We leave this chapter with the insinuation that Latino/a theology as such is limited in its *transformational mission*, hence needing to revise its assumptions about *culture* and the *nature of the church*.

Our second chapter challenges the dominant theological uses of culture, among several Latino/a theologians, which sees Latino/a culture as *locus theologicus*—a cultural perception that appears to be grounded on modern cultural (theological) anthropology. Proceeding with cultural suspicion and hope we are to ask *Is the modern cultural approach the most appropriate for Latino/a theologizing when confronting the reality of Latino/a heterogeneous culture and the reality of God as the historical transcendence Spirit?* If indeed, as we suspect, this is not the case, then we shall move to another cultural paradigm—with more *cultural capital* encompassing these two realities. We will venture to discern, then, a *Spirit-friendly* postmodern view of culture. By so doing, we hope to take the first step toward developing *Latino/a theology of culture* into a *Latino/a theology of the Spirit*—by identifying the church as the *cultural geography of the Spirit*.

Our third chapter builds on the second. If indeed the church is to be conceived as the geography of the Spirit of Christ, then *what matrices are formative in the making of the church, within history and culture, in a way that resembles the authorship of Christ's Spirit and the authenticity of human culture?* We aim here to finding the formative factors that conform a critical ecclesiology. We shall discern in the narratives of the Pentecost and the cross our ecclesial capital. We shall see how in the symbiosis of these two narratives the church originates and lives historically and culturally as God's communal transformational parlance.

Our fourth chapter represents our theological contribution. It does so in the *form* of a Latino/a ecclesiological construction, we call *the Mestizo/a community of Mañana*. Theologically, this construction represents the theological production of *Latino theology of the Spirit* and its dynamic methodology—a Pentecost-cruciform-shaped theology. Ecclesiologically, *the Mestizo/a community of Mañana* pretends to be a Latino/a ecclesiology from a postmodern perspective. Every formative element of this ecclesial construction (*mestizaje*, community/ *accompaniment*, and *mañana*) resembles a major theological development so far achieved within Latino/a theologizing. The chapter ends with a practical illustration based on the social praxis of *community organizing*. *Community organizing* shall help us demonstrate how the *mestizo/a community of mañana* can *walk with* Latino/a communities domestically as the embodiment of Jesus' transformative message, in the *form of* the cultural-ecclesial *practices* of Eucharistic presence, proclamatory presence, and pastoral presence.

A Word about the Terms Employed

As contextual theological language finds its place in American discourse, an effort to ease a clearer understanding of key terms is appreciated by audiences that are becoming contextual-friendly. In a spirit of welcoming those who are willing to explore contextual theologies, we shall provide with some beforehand clarification of a few terms and concepts that will be used with frequency in our coming discussions.

1. **Latino/a, Hispanic.** First, inclusion is one of the most important Latino/a theological values, thus words typically excluding women are modified or avoided, whenever possible. Latino/a

theology is a theology of woman, of the poor, of the children, of the family, of the weak, of the people. Second, our preference in the use of the term *Latino/a* over *Hispanic* is due to a couple of practical reasons. In the context of the author, Southern California, a growing Brazilian population is emerging. While the term *Latino/a* does not necessarily include them, the term *Hispanic* does exclude them on linguistic grounds—for *Hispanic* is directly identified with Spanish. Another practical reason for using *Latino/a* is that it resembles the creation of the Latino/a people not a "categorical imposition." In many settings the words *Latin@, Chican@, mestiz@* ("@" in place of "o/a") are being utilized to resemble inclusion. I am a major advocate of the idea that no term represents the richness and heterogeneity of the Latino/a people, yet, theological discourse requires such an invention.

2. **Mestizo/a.** We develop our understanding of the church around this concept in the course of our work—especially with regard to *mestizo/a* and *mestizaje*. Two things need to be mentioned here. One, the Latino/a informed reader will notice the absence of father Virgilio Elizondo as an explicit contributor in our understanding of the mestizo/a community of Mañana. He is mentioned on several significant occasions, but not as the main interlocutor on the topic of *mestizaje*. Father Elizondo's understanding of mestizaje is assumed and reconstructed in our work. Second, our use of mestizaje is subject to idealization and colonization—these symbolic risks are present and we assume them in our discourse. That said, our treatment of *mestizaje* hopes to extend beyond the understanding articulated by classical Latino/a theologians to incorporate a post-colonial/postmordern approach that recognizes the essential *otherness* that such a concept entails.

3. **Praxis, Practice.** *Praxis* is already loaded with Marxist and subsequently liberationist connotations. No matter what we do to it, it maintains its political, historical, and ethical baggage. *Practice*, in our context, refers more to the domestic realm, the cultural realm. On more than one occasion, however, we have used these terms interchangeably; the reader will know by context if such is the case.

4. **Holy Spirit, Spirit of God, Spirit of Christ.** We use these descriptions as a reference to the third person of the Holy Trinity. Centric to our theologizing is a dynamic-plurifom Christology, particularly a pneumatological Christology, which understands the Holy Spirit and the Spirit of Christ as one and the same in his missiological function. We provide in chapter three a critical note on this regard.

5. **Latino/a theology, Latino/a theologies, Latino/a theologizing.** We acknowledge the artificiality and pragmatic use of "Latino/a theology" as if one could accommodate the multiple perspectives, trajectories, and emphases of the diverse Latino/a theological community. For that matter, the description "Latino/a theologies," as De La Torre and Aponte indicate, is a more accurate alternative. In the course of this work, the reader will notice the insistence in the use of "Latino/a theologizing," which resonates with our particular view of theological production and the perspective from which we articulate our theological understanding. *Latino/a theologizing* points to Latino/a theology as a journey, as a process, as a repetitious narrative that contextualizes and prints its continuous character every time it is articulated. Latino/a theologizing refers to a critical faith that can be described and articulated, but not defined at one point only—in static terms. *Latino/a theologizing* is Latino/a theology-in-the-making, *a verb becoming a noun.*

The story about the Story of *Latino/a Theology of the Spirit*

Every theology is somebody's narrative. Any committed theologian hopes his/her narrative resembles God's narrative in people's life, although that is not always the case. I shall begin my story by telling you *where I am* in the trajectory of critical faith, this will tell you *who I am.*

As a Latino/a pastor doing ministry in the urban metropolis of Los Angeles, I am always on the road. For over a decade, I have been trying to get to the church but sometimes I find myself discouraged with heavy traffic. I come from a small port in the Caribbean North coast of Honduras, called *Puerto de Tela.* There was no traffic in *Tela,* that I remember. However, today I have to deal with Los Angeles traffic. The best way to cheat heavy traffic in the chaos of an urban metropolis such as Los Angeles is by becoming a *commuter*. So *I am a commuter*, for I am always on the road trying to get to the church. I have found that *commuting* is a *communal experience*. Although I learned to feel comfortable when driving my own car and listening to my own music and doing my own business while on the road, in Los Angeles commuting is the best way to go if I want to get to the church. Little by little, I have realized that I enjoy traveling in the *company* of others, instead of driving alone. In a sense, I am learning to deal with Los Angeles traffic in a *communal way*.

"My church" is made of more than 200 congregations that speak more than 22 different languages and represent more than 100 different nationalities. All of these congregations meet at a common crossroads— an American Baptist organization by the name of Los Angeles Baptist City Mission Society. I work there as a *regional minister* responsible for resourcing these congregations, so I travel a lot among uniqueness and diversity. I am always on the road to understanding: where is the church in relation to the Spirit's *aleteo* (fluttering), what conditions disempower and empower church ministry, and how is the Spirit moving the church as an agent of transformation across this challenging context? But in my daily traveling I face heavy traffic: ethnocentrism, modernism, fundamentalism, racism, liberalism, anti-charismatism, cultural intolerance, coerciveness, to name some. In order to deal with such a heavy traffic I *commute*. I have made of my ministry, as a regional church consultant, a *commuting ministry*. I am constantly taking people with me to the church, to experience diversity—the church multiple cultural-social-economic-theological locations. In so doing, I am becoming day by day a disciple of the Spirit, a cultural travel agent, and a ministry-forecast fan.

I have discovered that my life, as such, reflects *traveling* and *commuting* as a personal narrative. In a sense, I have learned to live a life *on the road*, a life *in between* the multiple locations I *commute* day by day. In my parish trajectory, I have been involved in theological education for ten years at Fuller Theological seminary. The Center for the Study of Hispanic Church and Community at *Fuller* has been a commuting home. At the same time, I've been involved with lay leadership training—at my local church and at some *institutos bíblicos* (bible institutes). So I am always commuting between the academy and the *church.*

In my own academic journey, I have found myself commuting between *faith* and *reason*, between *Jerusalem* and *Athens.* I have learned to travel between these *apparent* opposing realms. My experienced has been that *there is a life in between.* I have learned to cheat the traffic of Western modernism that told me that Jerusalem and Athens and that faith and reason are enemies. That might be the case for those only *living in* Jerusalem or in Athens or in faith or in reason, but I do not live there. I belong to the road of *faith seeking understanding.* On this road, reason and faith find yet another partner *sentimiento* (aesthetics). They all commute *with* me and *within* me by the grace of God and the power of the Spirit.

In my own cultural journey, I am always on the road. I came to the U.S. over two decades ago. Originally I thought I was no longer living in Latin America. I went to school while working at a mortgage company in an attempt to live the life of (at least) a middle class American. The idea was to make it in the U.S. So, the more Americanized I looked the easier the transition would be. But, I ended up discovering that Latin America was still living within me. In a weird way, Latin America was present as a historic memory. As I associated with other immigrant Latinos/as, I found they held a similar experience, so the historic memory became a shared social reality here at the heart of the U.S.

Now I know better. I live on the road. I am always *commuting* between the U.S. and Latin America. This is possible in Los Angeles for the world has been brought over here. I had the awesome experience of planting a Brazilian church in Los Angeles along with a fellow Brazilian pastor. During that time, I was able to mingle with Brazilians: playing soccer with them, singing with them, chatting with them, and especially eating with them. As I commute day by day, I am becoming culturally fluent amid the culture world traffic of Los Angeles.

Did I say I commute? Sorry, I mean *we commute*, my family and I. My wife is pretty much involved in church ministry (with me, and I with her). In order to finish school, we had to take turns given the financial challenges education represents for a Latino/a couple in the U.S. We also take turns in parish activities. Sometimes, while I am writing academic papers, she preaches and when I am preaching, she writes. It is an interesting yet challenging dynamic at times. With my son, who is a college senior, it is the same story. We have learned to educate ourselves on the road. We are commuters. I could go on and on talking about my story, but I am sure that by now my point is made.

   Latino/a theology of the Spirit is also a *commuting* story. The Latino Catholic theologian Roberto Goizueta sees the church as a *crossroads* where the home and the city meet.[3] In this sense, Latino/a theology of the Spirit is *crossroads theology*. As in my case, *Latino/a theology of the Spirit* constructs its views in the way *from* the church and *to* the church. It is essentially a practical theology of the Spirit, therefore, of the church. Given its commuting nature, *Latino/a theology of the Spirit* is concerned with the religious, historical, cultural, political, economic, and any item affecting Latino/a life as envisioned by God. *Latino/a theology of the Spirit* is aware of the heavy traffic congesting its various routes; yet it belongs to the road, it cannot do anything else but to *commute. Latino/a theology of the Spirit* is not "one-city theology." It belongs neither to Athens nor to Jerusalem, hence its fluid and postmodern*ish* style will challenge the more fixed theological paradigms and environments; yet it must roll on.

3. Goizueta, *Caminemos con Jesús*, 192.

1

Practical Theologies and the Call
for a Latino/a Theology of the Spirit

Practical Theology-in-the-making

PRACTICAL THEOLOGY IS BECOMING A CONTEXT WIDE DISCOURSE.
Several features have contributed to this phenomenon. First, practical
theology allows for diversity. For instance, when referring to practical
theology one finds that this discipline may point to *pastoral theology*
(Farley), *pastoral action* (Oden, Nadeau), a form of *theological ethics*
(Browning), or *ecclesial action* (Rahner, Anderson, Floristán).[1] Second,
although practical theology allows for diverse expressions of the same,
its methodological composition is common and resides in the binomial theory-practice (praxis).[2] Third, there is a growing consensus that
practical theology is about church action in the world. This particular
emphasis and common theological intention is expressed, for instance,
in terms of *theories of action*,[3] *theology of praxis*,[4] and *Christopraxis*.[5]
Finally, practical theology tends to be local and contextual. The fact that
practical theological approaches gear toward pastoral theology, liberation theology, and political theology underlines the strong ties practical
theologizing maintains with contextual issues.[6] In addition, academic

1. See Van Den Hengel, "Paul Ricoeur's Oneself"; and Heitink, *Practical Theology*,
esp. ch. 7.

2. See Floristán, *Teología Práctica*, 194–210. See also Heitink, *Practical Theology*,
110–23; Anderson, *The Shape of Practical Theology*, ch. 4.

3. Heitink, *Practical Theology*, ch. 9.

4. Floristán, *Teología Práctica*, 173–91.

5. Anderson, *The Shape of Practical Theology*, 132–34.

6. See Van Den Hengel, "Paul Ricoeur's Oneself."

rigor in practical theologizing is deemed as crucial as in "traditional approaches."[7] Critical reflection, as we have indicated, tends to be context-based and action-based and in dialogue with several interlocutors such as the church, tradition, the academia, and public life.

Due in part to different contexts and agendas, practical theologians may be said to manifest (at least) two movements when elaborating practical discourse: from theory to practice and from practice to theory. These movements describe, in our opinion, the immediate analytical framework from which these theologians exercise their discourses, while they maintain the primacy of practice (praxis) in relation to theory.[8]

From Theory to Practice: A Theoretical Framework for Practice[9]

In Germany, for instance, influential theologians such as Jürgen Moltmann and J. B. Metz with other pastoral theologians have "politicized" theological discourse and, in a way, have "renovated" the so-called pastoral theology.[10] This "renovated theology" has being invigorated by the binomial pattern "theory-practice" and the emphasis on ecclesial action as a forward movement beyond the self-edification of the church. More than *applied theology*, these theologians see practical theology as the critical reflection of ecclesial action in society. Herein, one of the main tasks of this practical theology is to verify the action of the church in society.[11]

In France and Canada, practical theology has taken a "sociocultural emphasis." R. Marlé and J. Audinet have proposed the "epistemological

---

7. We prefer the term "traditional" to "academic" for we understand "practical theologies" to be as critically rigorous and academically engaged, if not more, as disciplines such as systematic, historical theology, Christian philosophy, biblical exegesis, and so on.

8. Gerbern Heitink notices several shifts in the development of practical theology ending on praxis as the current location of practical theologizing. See Heitink, *Practical Theology*, 65. However, I am not referring to these evident historical-theological shifts but to the openness and weight theologians place on "praxis" as a self-revelatory space for reflection.

9. In this section, I follow Casiano Floristán's review of contemporary developments of practical theology. See Floristán, *Teología Práctica*, 162–71.

10. Ibid., 163–64.

11. Ibid.

rule" when elaborating theology. In this methodology the important question is not "how to do theological reflection" but "why"? Practical theologians, in this school, tend to use the paradigm theory-practice to produce a theological discourse able to "give an account of faith and the God this theology confesses within the context of social practices and cultural diversity."[12]

In Italy and Spain the dichotomy "doctrine-(pastoral) practice" has extended to the field of practical theology. Pastoral theology has been diluted into church practices without much (critical) reflection involved. Having acknowledged that, we must mention the impact of Latin American liberation theology on Spain. Some clerical and academicians have begun to revise theology and ecclesial action in dialogue with Latin American liberation theology. Spain is becoming, in the Spanish-speaking world, an important locality for the development of practical theology. Practical theologians such as Casiano Floristán and J. J. Tamayo have contributed to this fact, fostering an academic environment suitable for research and inter-contextual dialogue.[13]

In the United States of America, particularly in the Anglo-American theological context, there is a consensus that practical theologies have gone from a clinical-psychotherapeutic model of pastoral theology to an interdisciplinary-critical-ecclesial-action model.[14] Hiltner, Don Browning, David Tracy, among others, have contributed greatly to this field. Don Browning, for instance, develops his understanding of practical theology from the ethical-pastoral perspective operating methodologically with an understanding of the binomial theory-practice in terms of practical thinking or *phronesis*.[15] David Tracy tends to see practical theology as critical correlation of theory-praxis interpreted within the inner logic of the Christian truth and human situation. For Tracy the two main sources of practical theology are Christian tradition and human experience and language. Correlating both sources is the task of theology. Depending on the emphasis given in elaborating

12. Ibid., 167–68.

13. Ibid., 169–70. In addition, Floristán has been "there," at the genesis of and in dialogue with Latin American Liberation theology and U.S. Hispanic theologies. See, Juan José Tamayo, "In Memoriam," 155.

14. See Elaine Graham, "Pastoral Theology"; Floristán, *Teología Práctica*, 165–67; Heitink, *Practical Theology*, 115–23.

15. Browning, *A Fundamental Practical Theology*, 2–4.

this correlation, ecclesial action emerges as the self-actualization of the church or the construction of social reality (society).[16]

METHODOLOGICAL SHIFT

We have descriptively insinuated that practical theology as a discipline shows accentuated differences from traditional (academic) theologies such as historical theology, biblical hermeneutics, Christian philosophy, and systematic theology. These types of theological discourses have clear affiliations with formal (scientific) methodologies that prioritize theory over practice in the elaboration of theological discourse.[17]

Traditional theologies use theoretical-critical reason as a basis for inquiry and knowledge. Reality is grasped through a dialectic operation where objective data and interpretation produce understanding by following a method. This method, in Bernard Lonergan's words, is a "normative pattern of recurrent and related operations yielding cumulative and progressive results."[18] In this sense, theories are seen as containing objective understanding about a particular reality (the studied matter), which then are used to propose practices or action toward that reality. This has been, more or less, the way to construct theological discourse in the modern sense.

In which way is practical theology as a discipline different from traditional theologies? Three main differences, in our judgment, can be listed: methodology, location, and theological agenda.

16. Heitink, *Practical Theology*, 118.

17. Nancey Murphy labels "formal reasoning" that type of reasoning mostly used by logicians and mathematicians while "practical reasoning" that one used by theologians and Christian philosophers. See Murphy, *Reasoning & Rhetoric in Religion*, 5n.3. Although we recognize that logicians and mathematicians use formal logic as the basis of their theories, we contend that traditional theological education has taken a "formal character" and pursued formal discourse as a preferred mode of theologizing. Besides, from the Euro-American perspective, an "academic theologian" is expected to be an "academic thinker" utilizing an "academic-formal" argumentation when presenting his/her ideas. In the history of Christian thought the "way of attaining truth" has expressed in the battle between "reason and faith." Modernity, being Cartesian by nature, has favored "reason" moving theologizing into the location of the university hence moving theological language to "formal" discourse. A helpful discussion on this matter is found in the works of Austin Farrer. See for instance Farrer, *Reflective Faith*, and Farrer, *Faith and Speculation*. In addition see also Frank, *Philosophical Understanding and Religious Truth*, and Hancock and Sweetman, eds., *Faith & the Life of the Intellect*.

18. Lonergan, *Method in Theology*, 14–15.

With regard to theological method, practical theology includes critical or theoretical reason in the theological process but knowledge is not mediated by it. Instead, it is practical reason obtained from praxis which mediates truth. The primacy of praxis over theory does not undermine the role of critical reason for they co-exist in dialectical- mutual relation. Practical theologians differ in the way the binomial theory-praxis operates but would agree that the basic methodology of any practical theology must include an interaction between praxis and critical reflection, giving predominance to praxis in their methodology.

While traditional theologies have been produced from within the "academic environment" or "university," practical theology's first moment occurs in the context of ministry, culture, and society. This change of social location in theologizing constitutes, some argue, a clever move toward recovering theology as a *scientia practica*.[19]

Another distinction between traditional approaches and practical theologies is the emphasis on ecclesial action in the latter. Traditional theologies focus on particular fields of specialization: biblical studies, history, religion, Christian philosophy, etc. Hardly can one find a common agenda by which the truthfulness and reason of existence of these disciplines can be judged. Practical theologies, as Casiano Floristán has suggested, exist to apprehend (human situation), discern (critical inquiry), and act (church praxis) in the world based on (or in interaction with) the Word of God.[20] We discern here two different controlling passions. What moves traditional theologies is order, coherence, clearness of thought, distinctiveness, language, conceived within a given methodology. For practical theologies it is ecclesial praxis, action, context, concreteness in critical dialogue with reflection which shapes the theological agenda. While for traditional theologies the book is the product by which a sounding discourse can be judged, for practical theologies church praxis causes books to be written as expressions of communal practices.

19. See Maddox, "The Recovery of Theology."
20. Floristán, *Teología Práctica*, 201–3.

Illustration: Don Browning's Theological Movement from Theory to Practice

Don Browning's practical methodology might serve us to illustrate the tendency from theory to practice. Browning conceives practical theology as a fundamental theological discourse. That is, a theology that at the very core is critically practical and embraces other necessary theological discourses (descriptive, systematic, historical, strategic).[21] By practical, Browning means that any theology operates at its very core with practical reason. He describes the methodology of fundamental practical theology as theory-laden. He argues that "all practices have theories behind and within them." For this Browning makes use of practical philosophy and more particularly of the understanding of *phronesis*.[22] The concept of *phronesis* was elaborated createfully by Aristotle and followed up by contemporary thinkers such as Gadamer, Ricour, Habermas in addition to some American neo-pragmatist philosophers. Attempting a simplification, we could say that Browning presupposes that practical reason (*phronesis*) is at the core of human thinking. So the task of practical theology is to start with *phronesis*, then by using critical thinking *(theoria)* the theologian is to make sense of a particular *human situation* assisted by a range of specialized disciplines. Following, the theologian is to reformulate a practice/action *(techno)* that is congruent with the situation at hand.[23] For the above, Browning proposes a specific theological model to integrate practice and theory constituted by an "inner core" and an "outer envelope." In the *inner core* is the theologian who guided by practical reason asks two "ethical questions": *what then shall we do* and *how then should we live?* In the "outer envelope" the theologian interacts with four theological resources (inherited narratives and traditions) namely, interpretative paradigms, experiential probes, historical consciousness, and communities of memory.[24] Browning's theological process constitutes an illustration of a practical methodology with a tendency from theory to practice. That is, it presupposes *a priori* a practical rationality, which is indeed a theoretical framework "enabled" for human experience.

21. See Browning, *A Fundamental Practical Theology*, 34–54.

22. Ibid., 10–12.

23. Ibid., 34–42.

24. Ibid., 5–7.

From Practice to Theory: A Practical Framework for Theory

We present next two theological paradigms that point to a different movement (or inclination) in practical theologizing—from practice to critical reflection. First, Ray Anderson, a professor of theology and ministry with an evangelical background, will react constructively on Browning's paradigm suggesting that the praxis of Jesus Christ (in Scripture and through the church) is the most appropriate paradigm for church action in the world. Following, Latin American liberation theology, a well known movement originated from within the Roman Catholic tradition, will offer us a perspective that exemplifies how theology is done in the bipolar movement from praxis to theory. Both theological paradigms illustrate, in our opinion, how theology is a consequence of praxis.

RAY ANDERSON'S CONCEPT OF CHRISTOPRAXIS: FINDING JESUS' PRAXIS IN (DAILY) EXPERIENCE[25]

Anderson envisions theology as a practical discipline just as Browning and other practical theologians do. However, for Anderson two main axes define the essence of practical theology: the Word of God and the Work of God. Both axes are God's praxis in human context and define our task and role as practical theologians. From a human plane, the Word of God functions like a theoretical framework based on Scripture and maintains a critical dialogue with other disciplines. The Work of God, on the other hand, functions as a praxiological framework pointing to the praxis of Christ through the Spirit in the world. The Work of God illuminates the purpose of the Word of God. With this understanding in mind, Anderson proposes a corrective to Browning's model.

Anderson argues that Browning's model while valid for a practical theology within a postmodern environment presents two main deficiencies: a *Christological* deficiency at the core and a *Trinitarian* deficiency at the foundation. So Anderson attempts a reconfiguration of Browning's model by substituting in the inner core with a Christological component called *Christopraxis* instead of *experience—Christopraxis* means the continued presence and work of the Holy Spirit. Further, Anderson offers trinitarian components (Father, Holy Spirit, Son) that permeate

25. I am following Anderson's understanding as articulated in *The Shape of Practical Theology*. See especially chs. 2–4.

Browning's *outer envelope*. This trinitarian understanding intersects theological resources (inherited narratives and traditions) when developing a practical theology; not merely as cognitive categories but as revealing hermeneutical guides.

Ray Anderson, in his book *The Shape of Practical Theology*, shares a (ministry) case that moved him into the arena of practical theology. We will attempt to illustrate Anderson's modification of Browning's model noticing how a particular ministry praxis generates a particular practical theology.

Anderson shares the following case.[26] One of his church members, a woman who years ago had gotten divorced, met a man with the same situation. She, in order to learn what to do with regard to her present romantic relationship, sought pastoral counseling. She said to Anderson, "Pastor, I know what the Bible says about the law of divorce and re-marriage. I was not the innocent party in my divorce we were both guilty. I sought forgiveness from the sin of divorce and I have been forgiven by God. I know that by the Law in Scripture I cannot get marriage again. This man and I, however, love each other and love the Lord." So she asked, "Which side is God in our lives? Is God on the side of the law of divorce or is He on the side of the experience of forgiveness and love and marriage of his children?"

How would a pastor respond by using Browning's model? Browning's model would allow us to go either way. For example, the *human* situation question is can we re-marry? If the pastor and his/her congregation share a liberal moral posture—where human contentment is a primary factor and Scripture is secondary or subsequent in the criterion for action—the answer will be "yes." Browning's ethical question *what then shall I do?* can be used by this pastor to seek the answer in the *human* need of love and fulfillment and in liberal moral theory. Browning's ethical praxis of *how then should I live?* would be in part determined by that particular context, that particular congregation, and a perception of life as part of that *affirming* community. As a consequence, the pastor's praxis will find partners in dogmas, traditions, and other practices.

If, on the other hand, the pastor and his/her congregation share a fundamentalist morality—where the apodictic dimension of Scripture

26. Anderson, *The Shape of Practical Theology*, 13–14.

dictates the course of action—then a *literalistic* reading of Scripture would dictate something like the following response: "You know the answer already. You cannot remarry." Browning's ethical question of *what then shall I do?* would find in the experience of the interpreter—a fundamentalist pastor—and his/her corresponding community a support to his/her response. The ethical praxis that answers *how then should I live?* would find support in the immediate context, the dominant moral language, and the practice of this particular community. In this way, Browning's model could be used in both ways to say "yes" or to say "no." It is relativistic in character. Such a relativistic paradigm is shaped according to the dominant context, language, and communal perception of a given situation. This is why Anderson argues that Browning's model is valid within a postmodern context.

In Anderson's personal account, he responded with "Yes, you can re-marry." Anderson's Christopraxical model enabled him to find practical antecedents both in Scripture and in his church to act accordantly. However, Anderson's practico-theological axis—the Word of God and the Work of God—determined his ethical criterion. Since Anderson placed *Christopraxis* instead of *experience* in Browning's inner core, he sought *in the praxis* of Christ, as portrayed in biblical narrative, a paradigm for his pastoral action. First of all, he found a "historical antecedent" in Jesus' action interpreting the Sabbath. He, then, "discovered" an applicable principle based on Jesus' praxis as witnessed by Scripture. He was able to discern "Jesus' work" in this particular human situation, concluding that Jesus Christ is also the Lord of the law of marriage. Based on this hermeneutical process, Anderson provides a pastoral accompaniment in a way that is humanizing, affirming, liberating, and Christopraxical. The day when Anderson performed the marriage ceremony of this couple, he pronounced the following words in front of the church: "We are witnessing the *work of Christ*."

What we see here is a series of interpretative acts: the critical situation, Jesus' praxis, Scripture, and the purpose of human life under God. The congregation in itself was shaped and re-interpreted in light of this case. The phrase "we are witnessing the work of Christ" involves what Anderson would call a whole person's knowledge. We are participants in God's works not merely thinkers of God's words. *Participation* as *interpretation* (theological hermeneutics) is the essence of practical theology according to Anderson. This praxis is possible because Anderson is, first of all, a *participant* pastor involved in communal life. Second, and consequently, he is an *interpreter* theologian. This paradigm represents a movement from praxis to theory in the sense that "Jesus' work" is seen as present in this particular human situation. It is Jesus' work that caused reflection and theologizing. In a sense, Anderson's paradigm parallels liberation theology's paradigm. We turn next to liberation theological paradigm and its effects on the practical theological process in general.

LATIN AMERICAN LIBERATION THEOLOGY: MAKING SENSE OF GOD'S LOVE IN THE POOR

Since its origins, Latin American liberation theology has become a source for practical theology, offering a praxis-based framework for critical thought and historical-political praxis.[27] Christopher Rowland, Dean Ireland's Professor of Exegesis and Sacred Scriptures from Oxford University, asserts that liberation theology is one of the most influential movements of Christian theology in the last thirty years. It has dominated, declares Rowland, the intellectual framework of theologians for over a decade in universities and seminaries worldwide.[28] Although the genesis of liberation theology as a movement began in Latin America, parallel discourses around the world made liberation theology a worldwide theological idiom. The reason is evident, the experience of absolute poverty, injustice, marginalization, and human vulnerability affecting the poorest and marginalized regions of the world has urged for a concrete response from the Christian side. The hope for liberation from these conditions, in this case, is a worldwide cry.

Three decades after the emergence of liberation theology, Gustavo Gutiérrez offers a review where he reaffirms that liberation theology came out as an "effort to announce God as father in an inhuman world."[29] In view of the fact that the immediate challenge facing the Latin American context is one of poverty and injustice—where the poor is *invisible* and a *non-person* to the existing social, economic, and political order—continues Gutiérrez, then "how to tell these non-persons that they are God's daughters and sons" has been a primary concern for lib-

---

27. See Casiano Floristán, "Naturaleza de la Teología Práctica." See also, Heitink, *Practical Theology*, 51–65.

28. Rowland, ed., *La Teología de la Liberación*, 15.

29. Gustavo Gutiérrez, "Labor y Contenido," 52.

eration theology.[30] This announcement of God as father is, however, an ecclesial effort. It begins, says Gutiérrez, with an act of faith. A faith that, first of all, contemplates God while it is willing to obey his commands. Subsequently, liberation theology is an effort to reflect upon such an experience.[31] Gutiérrez calls this process a "first and second act" and constitutes the essential method of liberation theology. In this sense, liberation theology is understood as the "critical reflection on praxis in the light of the Word of God."[32] Gutiérrez clarifies, however, that this is not a method grounded solely on an ideology or social analysis, however novel it may appear. Neither is this theology manufacture-*able* within the confines of an academic setting, so to speak. Indeed, these "two moments, first and second acts," constitute a *lifestyle, a way of being a disciple of Jesus*.[33] Similarly, Leonardo Boff describes the methodology of liberation theology as follows:

> The condition of poverty of the immense majorities generated a commotion of Christian love . . . it became a true spiritual experience—the departing point for theology . . . Science, and in our case liberation theology, constitutes an effort for translating critically the rationality present in such a primal experience in terms of diagnosis, causality, processes and structural dynamisms, functionalities and tendencies there [experienced].[34]

For liberation theologians, then, liberation theology is a "language of God that, in ecclesial communion, seeks to make present the Word of life amid a context of oppression, injustice, and premature death."[35] Leonardo Boff, illustrates the liberation theological (practical) imagination of the church with the following words:

30. Ibid.

31. Ibid., 52–53.

32. The controversial term "praxis" refers, within liberationist thought, to "the conjunction of practices that gear toward the transformation of society," (Floristán, *Teología Práctica*, 176). In this sense, liberationist *praxis* extends the understanding of *Marxist praxis*—praxis after Marx took the connotation of a social-historical practice. However, liberationist theologians use such a term not innocently. That is, they reinterpret *praxis* in light of today's context and the Word of God. See Migueléz, *La Teología de la Liberación*.

33. Gutiérrez, "Labor y Contenido," 53.

34. See Boff, *Textos Selectos*, 195–96, my translation.

35. Gutiérrez, "Labor y Contenido," 63.

> THE CHURCH that becomes poor, even more, that allows the poor to feel [sentirse] Church, to the point of becoming the church of the poor with the culture of the poor, with their exploited condition (and denounced prophetically), with their way of celebrating Jesus Christ—who became poor (cf. 2 Cor. 8:9)—with the trust in the Holy Spirit, father of the poor, this kind of Church effectively becomes the sacrament of liberation and can present itself as bearer of the ministry of holistic liberation.[36]

In sum, theology of liberation is by definition critical reflection on historical praxis (experience) in the light of the Word of God, in communion with the church. It is critically praxical by nature. The primacy of praxis over theory is an evident attribute of this modality. Orthopraxis and not orthodoxy is the dominant force for ecclesial action in the public program of human emancipation (preferentially the poor).[37]

Liberation theology's practical imagination, as Christopher Rowland properly notices, has grasped the attention of influential theologians around the world. In our judgment, it represents a movement from practice to theory.

Conclusion

Practical theology is not just another theological discourse. It signals a paradigm shift in the process of theologizing around the world. Even though this paradigm shift is experienced differently in the many contexts out of which it emerges, this shift reveals that theology—in general—has gradually taken on a non-formal character, a character that is practical, communal, public, and domestic.

As this paradigm shift is adversely affecting the more traditional and formal theological approaches,[38] it is opening avenues for emerging theological discourses of the same practical genus to take their place in the academic, social, cultural, and public horizons of today's

---

36. Boff, *Textos Selectos*, 199, my translation.

37. See Gutiérrez, *Teología de la Liberación*, 189–226; Boff, *Textos Selectos*, 171–76.

38. Pedraja makes a good point in this regard. He observes that "philosophical and traditional" theological approaches are limited in their scope due in part to their dependency on formal reasoning. Such approaches do not represent life as it is and in a way truncates reality. See Pedraja, *Teología*, 83–84.

theologizing. Such is the case for Latino/a theology—a central theme in the next pages.

Liberation theology has contributed toward the *praxicalization* of theological discourse around the globe. In the same way, liberation theology has been instrumental in the parallel development of Latino/a theologizing. Some Latino/a theologians claim, "Latin American libera-tion theologians are one of the greatest influences on Latino/a theology."[39] It is a legacy and an ongoing theological protagonist. So our next task is to see how Latino/a theology emerges, similarly and encouraged by liberation theological discourse, out of the everyday struggles of the Latino/a people of the United States.

Latino/a theology as a Practical Theology of Culture

Latino/a Experience: The Beginning Point

Once I heard a Latino gentleman exclaiming recklessly, "Even though we might speak English with an accent, don't you dare believe we think with an accent." I said to myself, "I don't understand why this person is so angry at U.S. society, he should be grateful they have let him stay here. He must have an attitude problem; he's probably just a difficult individual." That incident happened more than two decades ago. I had just arrived in the United States, the "so-called promised land."

Now, my thoughts and feelings about the *other* have changed. Acculturation has taken place. Clashes of cultures have mingled to-gether within me creating a new perception of living, a new matrix of identity, a new set of cultural templates that yield to a better *mañana* (tomorrow) in *lo cotidiano* (daily experience). I no longer consider my-self a Latin American immigrant. Neither do I feel I exclusively belong within American society. Curiously, the "so called promise land" turned out to be a *diaspora*. Yet I do manage to live in both environments. I have learned to travel among cultures as a means to survival. Dominant American society, because of its dichotomous categorical language, seems to have a hard time understanding the possibility of multi-identity. Some claim that "multi-identity is not an accepted concept in U.S. dominant discourse. That discourse is about 'being for us or against us,' a black or white, Asian or white, *Other* or white . . . once placed in

39. Ibid., 35.

that category, the individual is assumed to possess all the characteristics of that category, good or bad."[40] So I have understood in my own experience what it means to be a Latino/a: a border-mestizo person living between the edge of cultural realities. In other words, my concrete existence within the U.S. entails a *being-in-between*—commuting from culture to culture, from experience to experience, from border to border, from story to story.

Making Sense of Latino/a Experience

"Latina/o experience and history," says the church historian and theologian, Justo González, is one "of conflict, violence, and oppression."[41] The fact that European ancestors invaded our lands, destroyed ancient civilizations, and sacrificed millions of natives in the process of expansion and exploitation is well known to Latinos/as. Europe has an interesting and rather mythical origin thinks González. It originated in Greek mythology when Zeus, in the form of a bull, raped "Europa," and thus is born what we will eventually be known as Europe. That is a myth. But not so is the origin of the New World. The raping, colonization, and exploitation of this new world are facts of history, tragic ones. However, this past history has become, in a sense, a *story* that tends to repeat itself in the sociocultural geography of the United States. So González goes on saying, our present "is also one of survival in the midst of brokenness, and joy in the midst of pain."[42]

In the past, some have suggested the term "internal colony" to explain the socioeconomic and political condition of the Latino/a people.[43] This is a term that, in the thought of Chicano sociologist Alfredo Mirandé, describes how a group of people ceased to have their own sociopolitical and economic power—having been forced into the political, economic and social power of another (dominant) group of people which is oppressive in nature. Mirandé's view suggests that by the mere fact of a person exhibiting linguistic, cultural or racial traits linking such a person to Latin America, this person is placed in the internal-colony-status better known as Chicano/a, Latinao/a, Mexican

40. Espinoza, "Latino/a Identity," 17.

41. Justo González, "Foreword," In *Teología en Conjunto*, ix.

42. Ibid.

43. Mirandé, *The Chicano Experience*, 188.

American, etc. Other Latino/a critics point to the fact that "even those who have been able to move up the economic ladder still experience prejudice and discrimination."[44]

Mirandé believes that the internal-colony-mentality is endemic to U.S. dominant culture's *modus operandi*. This mentality saturates the dominant stratus of social, economic, judicial, political (we add religious) structures. Thus the conviction remains—in the conscience of informed Latino/a sociologists, historians, and theologians—that there has been an intentional effort to keep the Latino/a people at the margin of the educational, political, economic, and religious processes of the United States.[45]

When we confront this marginalizing and oppressive sociocultural force with the unprecedented demographic growth of the Latino/a people and its diverse cultural matrix, we have a *community* whose stories are told in terms of struggle and survival amid a hostile environment that resists it. It is not surprising, therefore, that Latino/a experience

---

44. Ibid., ix–x.

45. For instance, in the matter of law and order, Mirandé observes, "Chicanos continue to receive differential and unequal treatment at the hands of the legal and judicial system." Behind this behavior against the Latina/o community, affirms Mirandé, is the "bandido (villain) mentality." This stereotype of Latinos/as as intrinsic lawbreakers permeates too much of the U. S. judicial and legal system. Education has been another mechanism of oppression for Latina/os. Mirandé maintains, "mind control is essential to colonization" (Mirandé, *The Chicano Experience*, 91). That is, education has been one of the means by which the dominant culture has achieved mind control over many Latinos/as along the years. Mental manipulation, through the advertisement of cultural assimilation as the only way to succeed in the U.S. society, has persuaded many Latinos/as to assimilate into Anglo-Saxon patterns of living till the point of passively accepting marginalization and oppression unto denial. Likewise, theologian, Justo González, an educator and academician, puts it more explicitly: "In schools, their culture and tradition are often not considered as worthy of study as are those that originated in Britain, France, or Germany. In many public schools, it has been traditional for Latino and Latina students not to be encouraged to prepare for college, but rather to be funneled into vocational schools." As a result, for decades a fact has remained constant in census figures: no matter how many Latinos/as there are in the nation, no matter how large the total population is, and no matter the changing trends in the economy, most negative indicators (unemployment, school dropouts, poverty) continue to hit the Latino/a community. González concurs with Mirandé in that there has been an intentional effort of keeping Latinos/as at the margin of the educational, economic, and political system. This marginalization and oppression has brought devastating consequences to the Latina/o community as well as to the diverse U.S. community in general.

affects Latino/a theology in a way that theologizing becomes a voice of/
for freedom, dignity, and hope.

The Nature of Latino/a Theologizing

Theologizing under these conditions requires *participation* and *commitment* with Latino/a *context*. Such a context is, first of all, one of constant growth. A person is said to be a "Latino/a" if he/she can trace his/
her ancestry to Latin America, the Caribbean, and even Spain in some
cases.[46] Latinos/as are the fastest growing segment of the U.S. population. They constitute a little more than 14% of the population, with over
44 million people—as of today the largest minority in the U.S.[47] Second,
the Latino/a context is one of poverty and sub-education, compara-
tively speaking. To be Latino/a, in many cases, means to be underpaid,
overworked, having no medical, retirement, or social security benefits.
Allan Krueger and Jonathan Orszag, in a research presented to The Pew
Charitable Trust in January of 2002 entitled "Hispanics and the Current
Economic Downturn: Will The Receding Tide Sink Hispanics?" report
the following:

> Despite the economic gains achieved by Hispanics in the 1990s,
> two areas of concern are prominent. First, Hispanics still lag
> behind the rest of the population along nearly every economic
> indicator. For example, the typical weekly earnings of full-time
> Hispanic workers ($396 per week in 2000) were just 67 percent
> of the weekly earnings of full-time white workers ($591 per week
> in 2000). In 2000, the white unemployment rate was 3.5 percent,
> compared to 5.7 percent among Hispanics . . . Second, the dra-
> matic gains among Hispanics during the 1990s may be tempo-
> rary. It is unclear whether Hispanics will be permanently better
> off because of the 1990s economic boom or whether their gains
> will be completely lost in the current economic downturn.[48]

Third, the Latino/a context exhibits a diverse religious matrix and spe-
cially one where popular religiosity is significant. Latino/a religiousity
encompasses a variety of religious practices and traditions among which

46. Delgado and Stefancic, eds., *The Latino/a Condition*, 1.

47. See Pew Hispanic Center, "Statistical Portrait of Hispanics in the United States,
2006." *Pew Hispanic Center*, 1/23/08. http://pewhispanic.org/files/factsheets/hispan-
ics2006/Table-1.pdf (accessed 10/03/08).

48. Krueger and Orszag, "Hispanics."

popular Catholicism and Protestant Pentecostalism/Charismaticism flourish. However, one must recognize the growing presence of cult religions: cult to the dead, witchcraft, Santeria, etc.[49] Fourth, the Latino/a context is a context of emerging generations. Pedraja points to the fact that:

> [C]oncerns about *Generation X* in the media and academic circles pale in comparison to those of *Generation Ñ*, a term coined by Bill Teck, whose parents are Cuban-Americans, to designate the thriving young Latino/a population who did not fit the rubric of *Generation X*. Studies indicate that 35 percent of Hispanics are under 18 years of age ...[50]

Latino/a pop culture has penetrated American culture through music, films, food, humor, art, and so on. Such cultural domains are still unreached domains yet to be explored by theological reflection. In sum, Latino/a multiple contexts reveal a kind of *Latino/a people* that struggle to survive yet it survives carrying within multiple stories of oppression, cultural diversity, poverty, emerging generations and a popular faith. The latter represents a voice of empowerment and hope. Hence, Latino/a theology emerges, as does liberation theology, out of the people's every day struggle for survival in an effort to give voice to the voiceless.[51] Consequently, to do theology from the Latino/a perspective is necessarily a consequence of this diverse, challenging, and concrete context.

Theologizing out of this particular context requires then a *collaborative* and *communal effort*. A Latino/a theology does not surface as an individual formal-academic project, however noble it may appear. The Latino/a context does not allow for such an extravagance. Luis Pedraja expresses it in the following way:

> Doing theology as a collaborative venture often takes the shape of an ongoing dialogue, a dialogue that engages different interlocutors. These partners in dialogue might be other Latino/a theologians, people from the church, communities, or the broader public ... Theology is not the possession of a few intellectuals, but the reflection and work of the community as a whole.[52]

49. See De La Torre and Aponte, *Introducing Latino/a Theologies*, 124–135.

50. Pedraja, *Teología*, 41.

51. De La Torre and Aponte, *Introducing Latino/a Theologies*, 43–53.

52. Pedraja, *Teología*, 71.

A Spanish phrase that captures this theological experience is "teología de conjunto" (theology in conjunction). Such a way of doing theology does not go without challenge. Doing *teología de conjunto* within the vast diversity characterizing Latinos/as naturally demands an unusual commitment toward the *other*. The Latino/a theological community, as we will learn throughout the development of our whole work, comprises different Christian traditions, races, social and cultural locations, ideologies, political stories, visions of the future, and theological emphasis. So elaborating Latino/a theology, *en conjunto*, has been a test of Christian virtue, character, and commitment. This test, to a great extent, has been successfully passed.[53]

Theologizing *in commitment, in context, and 'en conjunto'* has fostered an advantageous environment that draws together multiple disciplines. Consequently, Latino/a theology is also *interdisciplinary* in scope. In Latino/a theological discourses one finds traditional biblical-related disciplines such as historical theology, systematic theology, biblical hermeneutics, Christian philosophy, biblical languages, and so on. But also, in Latino/a theologizing one finds non-traditional disciplines and analytic tools such as cultural and theological anthropology, sociology of religion, aesthetic philosophy, ethnography, urbanology, homiletics, political theory, and literary criticism.[54]

Lo Cotidiano and the Theological Method

Lo cotidiano (daily experience), the beginning point of Latino/a theologizing, must be construed also as the culmination of the theological process. De La Torre and Aponte offer a concise and clear view of Latino/a theology as an articulation of the themes that represents Latino/a people's experiences and practices in *lo cotidiano*. Latino/a theology is, for the Latino/a Christian community, "the verbal expression of faith as practiced, believed, articulated, and celebrated by Hispanics."[55] Louis Pedraja adds that in the elaboration of Latino/a

---

53. It is very common to find collaborative efforts that reflect unity in the diversity we are referring to. See for instance, Rodríguez and Martell-Otero, eds., *Teología en Conjunto*; Espín and Díaz, eds., *From the Heart of Our People*; Isasi-Díaz and Segovia, *Hispanic/Latino Theology*; Aquino, Machado, and Rodríguez, eds., *A Reader in Latina Feminist Theology*.

54. See Pedraja, *Teología*, 66–75.

55. De La Torre and Aponte, *Introducing Latino/a Theologies*, 71.

theology (and any theology) one must take into account a multidi-
mensional matrix of reasoning. This matrix should entail theoretical
reasoning, practical reasoning, and aesthetic reasoning.[56] Theoretical
reasoning focuses on clarity, logical systems, accuracy, distinctiveness.
"While theoretical reason," argues Pedraja, "focuses on determining the
case and its search for 'truth', practical reasoning focuses on determining the right course of action with questions about what is right and
wrong, or what ought to be the case."[57] Aesthetic or poetic reasoning,
on the other hand, "seeks to determine the beauty, symmetry, and sub-
lime nature of something."[58] In this sense, aesthetic reasoning focuses on
symbols, cultural practices, artistic expressions and so on. This latter is
particularly useful in constructing, designing, and imagining realities in
interconnection with concrete experiences. In theological understanding we must use these three forms of reasoning, alleges Pedraja, for even
the most elemental statement of faith requires of such a matrix: "faith
seeking understanding."[59]

Lo cotidiano, in the Latino/a sense, exhibits indeed a merging of
action, *sentimiento* (feeling which in the Latino/a sense is a form of
aesthetic reasoning), and ideals. All of these categories, of every day
life, are experienced holistically and aesthetically within practices of
the community, music, humor, and religious celebrations. The practice
of life, in a Latino/a sense, cannot be understood as the sum of daily
activities or elements such as individual religious practices, individual
nationalities, single ways of social engagements, etc. These elements
and practices looked at one by one do not make much sense. Latino/a
life cannot be compartmentalized; it represents a type of *mestizaje* of
experiences, stories, struggles, and hopes.[60] When trying to understand
lo cotidiano, one will face a similar experience to he/she who looks into
a kaleidoscope. Such an experience entails the ability to appreciate the
one color and shape within the complex whole. It requires aesthetic ap-

56. Pedraja, *Teología*, 55–62.

57. Ibid., 58.

58. Ibid., 59.

59. Ibid., 60.

60. The term "mestizaje" is a central concept in this work, particularly in ch. 4, where
we will provide a much greater understanding. In this particular case, it refers to the
"mixture or mingling" of elements that have experienced a level of fusion yet maintain
distinctive characteristics—an otherness—that only make sense in conjunction.

perception. For instance, the so-traditional Spanish adages disclose a sort of popular ethics that perpetuate cultural customs and ideals. The famous *corridos mejicanos* (Northern Mexican country music) narrate, in a dramatic way, experiences of everyday life—which conjugate violence, actual plots, faith, and popular hope. This "informal" music genre, though originally rejected by the dominant artistic society (Mexican-Latin American), has managed to cross over sociocultural bounds finding a top place in the ethos of Latino/a art and the music industry. *La música regional norteña* (Northern Mexican country music) as of now is the most popular and profitable musical genre in the U.S. Latino/a world.[61] Why is it so? Perhaps because the story of many *immigrants* is told in popular style. The same can be concluded about the Latino urban twist *Reggaeton*—a unique mixture of Jamaican dancehall music, menacing gangsta rap, indelicate perreo (dog dance), all embedded in a socially-subversive and sexualized-lyric that tells the story of many Latino/a urban youth. Similarly, faith and religion is for most Latinos/as a matter of *everyday life*. Acknowledging this fact, the theological process must aim to penetrate Latinos/as' everyday life. De La Torre-Aponte explain:

> For Latinos/as, theology is more than dogmas or faith formulas; it is the daily articulation of faith in community, where it is known that God and the divine activity move and participate within history to save, liberate, and reconcile. In effect, theology becomes the reflection of God's praxis, God's action bringing about liberation from both corporate and individual sins. To do theology is to participate in the action of God.[62]

So De La Torre and Aponte conclude that Latino/a theology is "the Latino/a voice of faith."[63]

Methodologically speaking, Latino/a theology functions much like liberation theology, that is praxiologically. Given the hermeneutics of suspicion inherited from liberationist methodology, Latino/a theology takes issue on the so-called "objective concepts," therefore, to "know the truth" merely as a rational exercise is insufficient for Latino/a theologizing, thus the need for a more holistic epistemological apparatus.

61. See "Los Tigres Del Norte: La Reina Del Sur."
62. De La Torre and Aponte, *Introducing Latino/a Theologies*, 72.
63. Ibid.

From a practical theology perspective, Latino/a theology joins with those whose emphasis reflects an inclination from practice to theory. Here, De La Torre and Aponte elaborate precisely:

> Unlike many Eurocentric theologians, Latinas/os do not reduce praxis to a rational instrument of theory in which only verifiable praxis is relevant. Such reduction discredits alternatives like popular religion as relevant in the search for truth ... Latino/a theologians articulate a praxis-based theology that reflects the struggles of U.S. Hispanics.[64]

Clearly, liberationist methodology is normative for Latino/a theologizing as it is the liberationist theological intent or agenda. So argues De La Torre and Aponte, "the purpose of Latino/a theology is praxis, the *doing* of theology, known as orthopraxis (literally "correct action"), which is more important than developing abstract philosophical concepts about God."[65] The feminist Latina theologian María Pilar Aquino concurs with De La Torre and Aponte and adds, "Our aim is not new doctrines, but new relationships and lifestyles. Method implies a direction, and liberation is the direction."[66] Aquino understands that liberation begins by "infusing" a liberating vision into the people's life in the form of cultural and spiritual empowerment.

Illustration: Roberto Goizueta's Caminemos con Jesús

We could not possibly leave the topic of Latino/a theological methodology without mentioning Roberto Goizueta who has extensively written on this matter.[67] In our judgment, however, Goizueta's major contribution is not so much what he has written about theological method but his work *Caminemos con Jesús: Toward a Hispanic/Latino Theology of Accompaniment*, as a premier illustration of Latino/a theologizing.[68] Latino/a theological methodology is harmonious with the organization of *Caminemos con Jesús*. Goizueta dedicates the first two chapters to locate the Latino/a condition and experience within the context of

64. Ibid., 74.

65. Ibid., 73.

66. Aquino, "Theological Method," 23.

67. See for instance, Goizueta, *Caminemos con Jesús*; Goizueta, "U.S. Hispanic Mestizaje"; and Goizueta, "Liberation and Method."

68. See Goizueta, *Caminemos con Jesús*.

the U.S. Having identified his particular location, Latino/a popular Catholicism—the *locus theologicus*—he proceeds to analyse such an experience in light of multiple disciplines. The result appears in four chapters full of theological interaction with a variety of disciplines such as cultural anthropology, sociology of religion, aesthetic philosophy, Christian ethics, and urban theology. Such an analysis constitutes a fine work of practical theologizing and produces a "organic" anthropology that seeks to represent the Mexican American (popular) Catholic community. In his final chapter, Goizueta elaborates his "theology of accompaniment." This theology portrays ecclesial paradigms that are informed by a vision of Jesus as "compañero/a," and are designed to affect people's everyday life. The church is to *walk with* the marginalized and economically unprivileged incarnationally, as Jesus did, on equal basis and become an urban home (ethics, aesthetics, spirituality). In this way, Goizueta's theological journey begins in *lo cotidiano*, (daily experience) and aims to provide *liberating practices* capable of transforming people's everyday life.

Conclusions

Latino/a theologizing is contextual, collaborative, interdisciplinary, and domestic in intention. Besides, Latino/a theological methodology is evidently liberationist, where theological discourse is understood as critical reflection on popular practices. The emphasis, however, just like Christopraxis and liberation theologies more generally is one denoting a movement from practice to theory. Conclusively, then, Latino/a theology is practical theology in a fundamental way.

Latino/a theology's *locus theologicus*, the place where one finds God acting and revealing himself, is understood to be culture. Most Latino/a theologians in both traditions, Catholic and Protestant, seem to concur in the fact that culture is *where* Latino/a theology is most concretely grounded.[69] In this sense, Latino/a theology is people-based because it is culture-based. So Latino/a theology is *a (practical) theology of culture* also in a fundamental way. It seems, therefore, that in the intersection and commonality of both, liberating praxis and cultural

69. See Protestant literature such as Pedraja, *Teología*, 84; De La Torre and Aponte, *Introducing Latino/a Theologies*, 42–69; and Rodríguez and Martell-Otero, eds., *Teologia En Conjunto*, 11–19. Catholic literature would be even more explicit. See for instance, Aquino "Theological Method," 6–41; and Goizueta, *Caminemos con Jesús*.

analysis, Latino/a theology discerns God's praxis and God's language (theology). This process of discernment, however, assumes that God is *discernable* within the realm of these two realities, assisted by a set of interdisciplinary diagnostic tools. If this is so, we ask: under which conditions can "praxis" and "culture" correspond to God's self-revelatory conduits (God's praxis and culture) as evidenced, for instance, by biblical narrative, tradition, and today's popular religiosity? Latino/a hermeneutics of suspicion points to continuously revise our assumptions, sources, traditions, and practices in the light of God's love and justice in our present context.

A Plea for a Latino/a (Practical) Theology of the Spirit

Gustavo Gutiérrez portrays liberation theology as the result and consequence of asking and acting on the question *how can we speak of God as father in an inhuman world?* This question is about language. Yet, it cannot be *fully* answered based on a *formal* language, or a *grammatically correct* language, not even with descriptive or representational or metaphorical language or even speech-act language, however honoring and empowering it may sound. Let us not make a mistake here, all these theological dialects play a *defining* role in theologizing. In this sense, we praise Latino/a theologizing which—as *praxis-based theology of culture* and given its contextual, communal, interdisciplinary, and domestic nature—has succeeded in *describing* the historical, cultural, social, and religious location of the Latino/a people in the context of the United States. Latino/a theology has also succeeded in *representing* the Latino/a communities' defining struggles and hopes through its theological language. But in spite of these achievements, Latino/a theology is yet required to continue moving in the direction of a *transformational* (domestic) discourse. In other words, Latino/a theology must continue to strive for the kind of language of God that Gutiérrez' tradition continues to struggle for.

Justo González, one of the pioneers of Latino/a theology, articulates our concern more pointedly:

> Professional theology is by nature elitist and therefore classist
> ... No matter how much we may regret it, most of what has been
> published ... is elitist. This is probably the most difficult chal-
> lenge of the next decade—indeed of the next millennium. Will

> we learn to listen to the wisdom of babes, of the uneducated
> Salvadorian refugee, of the old man who sits quietly on a pew in
> our church? And will we learn to translate our speech in such a
> way that in it the freeing gospel of Jesus Christ may be heard by
> the least of God's babes? We have shown that we can do theol-
> ogy with the "best" and the "great"; will we be able to do it with
> the least and the last who are God's first?[70]

What needs to happen theologically to speak the language of the people
we are *committed* to, *belong* to, *share life* with, and seek to *serve*? Is it our
call as theologians of the Latino/a people to understand, participate,
describe, and represent and do it excellently and in a way that dignifies
our people in the theological and social table and political table? Or
should we continue to dream, to imagine yet a *more subversive praxis*,
one where multiple powers intersect—spiritual and material, cultural
and political, communal and personal, academic and domestic, present
and future—encountering people's everyday practices and empowering
them to become embodiments of God's love and peace? Should we not
seek for such a praxis even though such a quest might challenge our
very *primal concept*, that of culture, that of community, that of church
in order to speak in the people's own tongues as if we were God's eschatological *nãvi* (prophet), as if we were the *Pentecost* community?

Latino/a Theology of the Spirit as a Theology of Cultural Renewal

In order to announce God as father in an inhuman world, let us become
the *cultural vessels* of the Spirit. For, as the Apostle Paul reminds us,
"we have this treasure in clay jars, so that it may be made clear that this
extraordinary power belongs to God and does not come from us" (2
Cor 4:7). The kind of language that is able to *announce God as father in
an inhuman world*, is not a human-originated language—this endeavor
is futile. That kind of language originates in God's self-community, the
holy trinity, and is articulated in us by his own Spirit. "And because [we
are his] children, God has sent the Spirit of his Son into our hearts,
crying, 'Abba! Father!'" (Gal 4:6). A theology that acknowledges and
gives a place to such a linguistic phenomenon is able to break through
any cultural boundary, political structure, colonizing discourse while

70. Quoted in Rodríguez, "On Doing Hispanic Theology," 19.

penetrating in people's domestic spaces, *lo cotidiano*. Latino/a people have learned to cry for freedom and justice. Latino/a theologians should become, more and more, a community of the Spirit who guide our people to learning the most *subversive language ever*, spirituality. Latino/a spirituality is God's language in *lo cotidiano*, through which "the Spirit helps us in our weakness; for we do not know how to pray as we ought, but that very Spirit intercedes with sighs too deep for words. And God, who searches the heart, knows what is the mind of the Spirit, because the Spirit intercedes for the saints according to the will of God" (Rom 8:26–27).

In the following pages we make a plea, then, for a *Latino/a theology of the Spirit* that sees culture as *locus theologicus* when such a culture encounters the Spirit of Christ. Consequently, "culture" is not understood as a monolithic, homogeneous, self-consistent complex whole at the mercy of theological categorizations for sake of a theological discourse, however dignifying and liberating it may appear.

Latino/a Theology of the Spirit as a Pentecost-Cruciform theology

In order to announce God as father in an inhuman world, let us envision the church of the Pentecost which is the church of the cross. The always-emerging, heterogeneous, and self-inventive character of Latino/a religiosity demands for a vision of the church that is able to embrace such a complex flux. A vision of the Latino/a church is needed that while *reflecting* the traits of the New Testament church also *refracts* the evolving, diverse, and eschatological character of Latino/a communities. In light of this, the narrative of the Pentecost and the cross continue to be today God's formative biblical means for authoring Christian experience and forming Christian community. The Spirit of God is the cruciform Spirit—the maker of the Christian community, Jesus' everlasting culture. The Latino/a church shall be perceived precisely as such, the resurrected body of Christ, resurrected culture. Leonardo Boff has boldly anticipated such a vision: "The Church . . . forms the resurrected Body of Christ. She is *body*, not in the sameness of Jesus' fleshly body, but in the sameness of his [Jesus] pneumatic (resurrected) body."[71]

---

71. Boff, *Jesucristo el Libertador,* 227.

In the following pages, therefore, we will imagine the Christian community as a Pentecost-cruciform community. Such a community represents a cultural geography where the Spirit of the resurrected Jesus continues to act and think, historically and concretely, in and through the Church.

Latino/a Theology of the Spirit as a Transformative Ecclesial Discourse

In order to announce God as father in an inhuman world, finally, let us become the theologians of the Spirit. Let us use our 'Latino/a' theological imagination to paint and imagine a Latino/a church that resembles inclusiveness, a communal self, and the appropriation of God's promises of *mañana* (tomorrow) as today's realities. Let us speak no fatalism, let us proclaim no pessimism, so let us see the cross in the light of the power of Pentecost. Let us seek Pentecost with the commitment of the cross. The language of authentic transformation—a rhetoric of love, joy, and hope—is the language of the *historical-transcendent* Spirit of Christ amidst the Christian community. Virgilio Elizondo one of the *founders* of Latino/a theologizing articulated this vision superbly:

> There will be a *new language*, truly universal: the language of *agape*. It is the language of selflessness in the service of others, the language of the radical acceptance and love of the other as other. It is a language of the heart, communicating directly with others regardless human differences. The Spirit begins the work of *transformation* with Jesus' apostles.... All are invited, but they must open their hearts to the *influence of the Spirit* in order to be converted to the new way of life preached and inaugurated by Jesus.[72]

Such a transformational language is able to empower the Latino/a church for accompanying the Latino/a community *Christopraxically.*

In the process of imagining a church like the one just described, we will revisit appreciatively and critically several foundational concepts typical to Latino/a theologizing. So in the next chapter, we will focus on the concept of culture and its theological uses. We will explore the way in which Latino/a theologians use culture as *locus theologicus,* imagining creative ways in which theologizing can be articulated

---

72. Elizondo, *Galilean Journey*, 83, emphases added.

relevantly when facing current postmodern contexts and today's Latino/a heterogeneous realities.

2

Latino/a Culture and the Spirit: Toward a Spirit-Friendly Postmodern Perception of Culture

IN THE PREVIOUS CHAPTER, WE INTRODUCED LATINO/A THEOLOGY AS a praxis-based discourse, which emerged as a contextual, collaborative, interdisciplinary, and domestic articulation of the Latino/a faith. Latino/a theological methodology is fundamentally practical or praxis-based, hence, Latino/a theology is "critical reflection on popular religious practices." Its prophetic task has revolved around three things: (1) understanding the U.S. Latino/a context, sociocultural location, and popular religious practices of the Latino/a people; (2) re-reading the biblical narrative from the specific Latino/a-location; and (3) advocating for cultural liberation and emancipation (e.g., by crafting an inclusive theological language that resists any type of oppression based on race, gender, social class, and alike).[1] Given its praxis-based methodology and its primary location (culture), Latino/a theologizing is elementally *a practical theology of culture*. As such, we concluded, Latino/a theologizing has successfully been *descriptive* and *representational* yet requiring more of a *transformational* genus. In light of this, we proposed that transformation is about a language that is divine in origin but cultural in practice. In the present chapter, we claim that Latino/a theology can continue moving toward a *transformational discourse*—one that culturally witnesses to Jesus—by expanding its modern understanding of culture to include the historically transcendent Spirit of Christ.

In the following pages, therefore, we will concentrate on the concept of culture as commonly understood by influential Latino/a theologians. Culture, we will see, is *where* Latino/a theology is most concretely grounded. Because of this fact, our task will take us to finding the proper

1. See De La Torre and Aponte, *Introducing Latino/a Theologies*, 43.

theological and cultural approach by which Latino/a culture, as *locus theologicus,* can correspond to God's self-revelatory cultural geography. While it is true that some influential Latino/a theologians resist postmodern perspectives of culture in view of a more manageable and immanent understanding, one that assumes that (Catholic) religion is a concrete universal underlying Latin/o culture as a whole,[2] others have begun to engage critically with postmodern views in the service of a more relevant and ecumenical perspective.[3] We subscribe to this latter position.

We will proceed by understanding *how* and *why* Latino/a theologizing came to see culture as a primary location for theologizing. So, beginning with Latino/a theology and its developmental stages, we will then reflect on how influential Latino/a theologians use cultural themes in their theological language. Here, we will highlight the impact of modern anthropology on Latino/a theologizing, concluding that Latino/a theologizing has been operating with a modern understanding of culture in mind.

Secondly, we move toward a wider dialogue on the matters of culture, examining cultural postmodern perceptions and challenges as presented by Kathryn Tanner, Tomoko Masuzawa, Robert Schreiter, and Régis Debray in the interest of displaying the limitations of theologizing with a modern cultural understanding in mind.

Finally, Alex García-Rivera and William Dyrness guide us toward an understanding of culture that can incorporate the historical transcendent Spirit of Christ by integrating a theology of creation into a postmodern language. We trust this effort will help us expand the frontiers of *Latino/a theology (of culture)* to embracing a *Latino/a theology of the Spirit.*

2. See Aquino, "Theological Method in U.S. Latino/a Theology"; Goizueta, *Caminemos con Jesús,* ch. 6. Justo González can be named here insofar as one understands that he is in favor of an alternative Latino/a version (of postmodernity) he calls "metamodernity." See González, "Metamodern Aliens."

3. See Segovia, "In the World but Not of It"; García-Rivera, "Creator of the Visible and the Invisible"; Recinos, "The Barrio as the Locus of a New Church"; and Vásquez and Marquardt, *Globalizing the Sacred*; De La Torre and Espinosa, *Rethinking Latino(a) Religion and Identity.*

Culture as the Primary Location of Latino/a Theologizing

Socio-Theological Development of Latino/a Theologizing

Latino/a theology is almost four decades old. This theological articulation, as we have stressed before, is a collaborative theological discipline; always-emerging, always-engaging the culture-making process, and always-seeking human affirmation, justice, and community. Any one attempt to define this discourse as final would fail, so we are better off describing it as a journey of commitment and critical faith.

As indicated in the previous chapter, Latino/a theology has emerged as a socio-culturally located discourse within America in concurrence with one of its older sisters, Latin American liberation theology.[4] The works of Eduardo Fernández, De La Torre and Aponte, Rodríguez and Martell-Otero, among other works, have sketched social-historical-theological frameworks for understanding the development of Latino/a theology in the United States.[5] Drawing from such portrayals one can recognize that a number of voices have contributed to different levels of construction of Latino/a theology during these decades. For practical purposes, we organize them into three categories according to their theological originality and the influence these voices have exercised on other theologians. As a disclaimer of our categorization—as of any— this grouping reflects our particular perception of representative public figures or academicians that have stamped Latino/a theology with their particular writings. By no means do we deem our typology to be exhaustive. We acknowledge the fact that many, perhaps most significant contributors pertaining mostly to the oral tradition, have been left

---

4. See Aquino, "Theological Method in U.S. Latino/a Theology," 15. Also Gilbert Cadena attempts a side-by-side comparison between Latino/a theology and Latin American liberation theology in "The Social Location of Liberation Theology."

5. Our analysis is directly informed by the following major works: Rodríguez and Martell-Otero, eds., *Teología En Conjunto*; De La Torre and Aponte, *Introducing Latino/a Theologies*; and Fernández, *La Cosecha*. We do acknowledge, however, numerous other contributions on this subject. See, for example, García, "Sources and Loci of Hispanic Theology"; and Aquino, "Directions and Foundations of Hispanic/Latino Theology." These articles in a way settled the foundations of the *Journal of Hispanic/ Latino Theology*, one of the finest sources of Latino/a theological discussions. Also, the work of Allan Figueroa Deck is seminal in this matter. See Deck, *The Second Wave*.

aside. Having said that, we think of three representational groups in the development of Latino/a theology: *founders, builders,* and *shapers.*

FOUNDERS

Though the true authors of Latino/a theology are the many Latino/a communities, which constitute Latino/a context, founder theologians can be said to break the ice and set the pace for future developments of Latino/a theology. For instance, Virgil Elizondo, Justo Gozanlez, and Orlando Costas come to mind in this category.

Virgil Elizondo is considered by many Latino/a Catholic theologians as "the father" of Latino/a Catholic theology. He has been a prolific writer responsible for over fifty titles including books and articles relating to Latin/o theology.[6] Among his most popular works are *The Galilean Journey* (1983) and *The Future Is Mestizo* (1988). Being Roman Catholic and Mexican-American in origin, Elizondo engages in a self-identity struggle, finding himself in distress by having to live between two cultural worlds. This existential stance moves him to seek academic tools to understand and explicate his paradoxical living condition, that is, living at the edge of two cultures—Mexican and Nordic American. Such a cultural paradox—Mexican and Nordic at the same time—is captured in Elizondo's concept of *mestizaje.* Mestizaje, referring here to a merger of two cultures in one person's life experience, permeates Elizondo's entire theological understanding and marks Latino/a theology. Mestizaje becomes for Elizondo a key Hispanic hermeneutical metaphor to reading Scripture, understanding anthropology, and seeking justice in society. Jesus Christ is portrayed, in *The Galilean Journey* for instance, as the mestizo par excellence. He is the culturally-marginalized-oppressed half-breed Galilean figure who is, nonetheless, the chosen one of God to liberate his people from bondage. This place in life is a status Latinos/as share with Jesus of Nazareth.[7]

Another *founder* is the Puerto Rican Orlando Costas, who influenced Latino/a theology from an evangelical perspective. With an American Baptist background, Costas was enchanted by the significance of missions in doing theology. He maintained, for the most part, a critical dialogue with Latin American liberation theologians yet struggled

---

6. See Fernández, *La Cosecha,* 38–39.
7. See Elizondo, *Galilean Journey,* chs. 4 and 9.

in contextualizing theological discourse to conform to the issues of America. Costas' contribution to Latino/a theologizing is in the fields of missiology, Christology, and ecclesiology. Some of Costas' key writings are *Christ Outside the Gate* (1982) and *Liberating News: A Theology of Contextual Evangelization* (1989). Costas emphatically stresses the fact that every theology is contextual theology. Costas develops a missiological type of Christology. For Costas the salvific action of God happened at the periphery of dominant religious structures in the time of Jesus of Nazareth. Jesus of Nazareth grew up, exercised his ministry, died, and was resurrected outside the gates (beyond the boundaries of formal religion-culture). The church must, in Costas' view, follow the example of the Jesus of the periphery. Although living at the margins of the dominant society-religion-culture, the church must be a church that is committed to do missions contextually from the margins, just as Jesus did.[8]

A third *founder* is the Cuban born church historian and theologian Justo González. González is perhaps the most respected Latino/a theologian among and beyond Latino/a circles. His privileged education at Yale, his prolific writings, and his ambitious theological education vision has granted González a position of respect and leverage among American academic elites. He has used this influence for the advancement and development of Latino/a theology. González's main field of expertise is historical theology. He has used his expertise to confront myths surrounding the historical interpretation of Christian doctrines. González has made clear that doctrines *have not* developed historically in a sociological vacuum. Thus, the "politicization of doctrines" has been exposed by. As well, González has emphasized the need for Latino/a theologians to re-examine and re-interpret Christian truths in the light of the Latino/a context.[9] He has served as an academic architect at the foundational moment of Latino/a theology, pointing out doctrinal deficiencies as well as invented academic mechanisms to enhance the emergence of a Latino/a community of scholars that would carry on the task of contextual theology for the Latino/a community of the United States.[10] Among his numerous writings are works such

8. Costas, *Christ Outside the Gate*, 188–94.

9. That is, Latino/a theologians do not host an "innocent reading" of the Bible and theology. They read them with "Hispanic eyes." See González, *Santa Biblia*.

10. Justo González has been responsible for influencing the Pew Charitable Trust and the Fund for Theological Education, among many other educational agencies, in

as *Mañana: Christian Theology from a Hispanic Perspective* (1990) and *Santa Biblia: The Bible through Hispanic Eyes* (1996).

BUILDERS

The builders are the next level of Latino/a theologians. They generally elaborate on foundation established by the founders, adding to it material content and practicality. Here we find the works of the Jesuit Allan Figueroa Deck, who provides a pastoral/practical platform for doing Hispanic ministries in the context of U.S. America, particularly among Roman Catholics.[11] Also Orlando Espín falls into this group, providing a light on the subject of popular religiosity and gearing toward a Roman Catholic systematic theology from the Latino/a perspective.[12] Most theologians of the Academy of Catholic Hispanic Theologians of the United States (ACHTUS) can also be grouped in this category. Latina theologians such as María Pilar Aquino, Daisy Machado, Jeanette Rodríguez, Yolanda Tarango, and others have been able to build a feminist theology from a Latina perspective.[13] In the Protestant sphere, we include theologians such as Eldin Villafañe who builds a platform to develop a Latino/a urban ethics from a Pentecostal perspective.[14] Samuel Solivan who has been a pioneer in working on Latino/a pneumatology also works from the Pentecostal/Charismatic perspective.[15] Elizabeth Conde-Frazier has worked on issues pertaining to Latino/a Spirituality and theological education among non-formal ministry-training centers (the so-called Bible institutes).[16] Ismael García is another builder whose emphasis on moral ethics, from the Hispanic perspective, allowed him to develop ethical views that portray the church as a moral

---

favor of Latino/a theological education. The *Hispanic Summer Programs, La Asociación para la Educación Teológica Hispana* and *The Hispanic Theological Initiative* are but institutional testimonials to his unceasing commitment toward Latinos/as' theological education.

11. See Deck, *Second Waves*; and Deck, ed., *Frontiers of Hispanic Theology*.

12. See Espín, "Grace and Humanness."

13. See Aquino, Machado, and Rodríguez, eds. *A Reader in Latina Feminist Theology*.

14. Villafañe, *The Liberating Spirit*.

15. See Solivan, "The Holy Spirit"; and *The Spirit, Pathos and Liberation*.

16. See Conde-Frazier, *Hispanic Bible Institutes*; and Conde-Frazier, "Hispanic Protestant Spirituality."

agent in society and a community of resistance against oppression and marginalization.[17]

SHAPERS

Finally, we think of *shapers* as those who further define areas of Latino/a theology and give them a peculiar *rostro* (face) or *style*. Some might argue that this category of theological construction reflects a production "out of" previous Latino/a theological concepts (*ex latino/a*). That might be the case, but as we will argue later it is not the "what" but the "how" that prevails in a Postmodern context. Indeed, these theologians have taken advantage of previous developments in order to provide a *finishing touch* to one or more aspects of Latino/a theology in a way that is *engaging* and *hospitable* to Latino/a communities. Four theologians come to mind in this category. Fernando Segovia and Harold Recinos are coloring outside the box by beginning to theologize *latinamente* from a postmodern perspective. Ada María Isasi-Díaz and Roberto Goizueta bring *lo cotidiano* (daily experience) to the center of their theological task.

For instance, Harold Recinos, elaborating on Costas' contextualization view and liberationist critique on social structures, has been able to re-imagine the church based on the experience of life in the *barrio*. He develops the notion of the "New Barrio Church," a church that is a consequence of *barrio life* but at the same time is able to change several conditions of life within such an urban context. Recinos views *locus theologicus* in fluid and dynamic ways not necessarily defined by one-universal cultural core but by muliple experiences that form the identity of that particular barrio.[18]

Fernando Segovia, similarly to Recinos, sees that communal identity is very complex and in constant flux, admitting the multiple matrices that shape identities within a community. So Segovia imagines a "diaspora theology," one that sees "exile" as *locus theologicus* and "journey" as the main *theme*. Herein, theologizing is postcolonial/postmodern in nature and—by delineation—the theological task encompasses

---

17. See García, *Dignidad*.

18. See Recinos, "The Barrio as the Locus of a New Church."

an "inductive, contextual, and pluralistic" methodology, *liberating* in intent.[19]

Isasi-Díaz is popular for utilizing ethnographic analysis as a way of grasping the life experience of Latina women. Functioning as a cultural map, ethnographic analysis focuses on the particularities of ordinary life as portrayed by Latinas themselves.[20] The result is *Mujerista* theology, a discourse that alleges to be people-based or *popular discourse.* Isasi-Díaz has taken a bold move toward a specific aspect of Latino/a theology, one that addresses women's every day struggles with the intention of dignifying the effort average Latinas exercise day by day, namely, *survival.* By using theology as a way of bringing out the life and voice of the Latina woman, Isasi-Díaz has provided a peculiar *rostro* or *style* to Latina theologizing, *un rostro mujerista* (a mujerista theological face).

Roberto Goizueta, discussed in the last chapter, on the other hand, worked for years in issues pertaining to theological method culminating in the fine volume, *Caminemos con Jesús: Toward a Hispanic/Latino Theology of Accompaniment.* Since Goizueta's paradigmatic concept of *accompaniment* is central to the present work, we will revisit Goizueta's work more thoroughly in subsequent occasions. It is enough here to designate Goizueta a *shaper* since he has been able to paint a *rostro* of Latino/a theologizing where the ecclesial praxis of *accompaniment* can stimulate Latino/a ecclesial action in general, for Catholics and Protestants alike.

In conclusion, these typologies could help us locate ourselves in the social, cultural, and theological journey of Latino/a theologizing. As we will see, these representations are not fixed and/or progressive in a lineal way. For instance, though Justo González and Virgil Elizondo are portrayed as *founders,* they continue to build and shape Latino/a discourse, exploring fresh, relevant, and foundational concepts.[21] Furthermore, we could be witnessing a new generation of *reconstructing theologians* who see a need, as the present work argues, to rethink, revise, and re-imagine

---

19. See Segovia, "In the World but Not of It."

20. See Isasi-Díaz, *En La Lucha/in the Struggle,* 65–79.

21. For instance, see González's eschatological concept of *mañana* in González, *Mañana*; and Elizondo's view of *Guadalupe* as the formative matrix for *mestizaje* or new creation in Elizondo, *Guadalupe.*

Latino/a religious discourse and identity as a whole without losing distinctive Latino/a roots.[22]

Discerning Theological Uses of Culture among Latino/a Theologians

Discerning a common cultural understanding among Latino/a theologians is a challenging endeavor. Diversity, as we have seen, is at the essence of what it means to be Latino/a and to think *latinamente*. Indeed, the phrase "Latino/a theologies," used by Miguel De La Torre and Edwin Aponte, is perhaps the most accurate way to speak of Latino/a theologizing. Nonetheless, the Jesuit Eduardo Fernández ventures to take the challenge of surveying an assorted and influential group of Latino/a theologians in his work *La Cosecha*. In search of a discernable node between culture, context and theology among Latino/a theologians, Fernández employs the theological models of contextual theologies as conceptualized by Stephen Bevans in his work *Models of Contextual Theology*. Bevans' particular interest in contextual theologies—how faith and culture interact—offers Fernández five ways to categorize Latino/a theologians. Put shortly, Bevans distinguishes five theological methodological emphases when dealing with contextual theologies: (1) the *translation model* has to do with making the "unchanging Christian message" available in a given culture; (2) the *anthropological model* focuses on how the Christian message integrates into culturally constructed identity; (3) the *praxis model* deals with the transformation of culture by its confrontation with the Christian message; (4) the *synthetic model* methodology rests upon the integration of cultural identity and social change, thus it is a composite of the *anthropological* and *praxis* models; finally, (5) the *transcendental model* focuses on knowing and acting within a particular community or context.[23]

Fernández is conscious of the fact that Bevans' models are an artificial hermeneutical apparatus for categorizing complex theological methodologies. Besides, Latino/a theologians' methodologies are multiple and sometimes complex. That being acknowledged, Fernández observes that Latino/a theology in general oscillates between the

22. See, for instance, De La Torre and Espinosa, *Rethinking Latino(a) Religion and Identity*.

23. Bevans, *Models*, 30–110.

anthropological model and the *praxis* model. However, Fernández's review points to the fact that the *anthropological model* seems to take priority over the other four models in the development of Latino/a theologizing in the U.S. in the past three decades. Fernández remarks:

> Deck has commented that because of the dire socioeconomic situation of the poor in Latin America, liberation theologians have chosen a more explicitly liberation-oriented mode. However, in the United States, as previously stated, Deck concludes that "Hispanic theologians have gravitated toward *cultural* analysis, especially to popular culture as epitomized by popular religiosity . . . the focus he is referring to, therefore, is more anthropological.[24]

Robert J. Schreiter in his review of the development of Hispanic theology also recognizes the centrality of anthropology in the theology-making process from the Latino/a perspective. However, he admits that "Hispanic theology's focus upon themes of liberation cannot be discounted."[25]

Taking these observations into consideration, it seems to us that *founders* and *builders* have provided a solid anthropological platform during the last three decades on which more recent generations of Latino/a theologians (e.g., *shapers*) have begun to *draw* a more specific, distinctive, and practical theological *rostro* for the Latino/a community. If these observations are true, the *anthropological impulse*—that understands *culture* as diverse yet possessing a universal inner core—in Latino/a theological beginnings was a necessary step toward a more fluid, contextual, and domestic theology to emerge in future generations.

In the following pages we will provide a brief review of cultural-anthropological themes as articulated by influential Latino/a theologians, venturing to argue that most of Latino/a theology has been developed from a *modern anthropological-cultural* perspective. We are not the only ones who have noticed this *modern cultural* tendency. Robert Schreiter explains:

> [I]t would be safe to say that much of the literature of Hispanic contextual theologies reflects a modern sense of the concept of culture. This is to be expected, since those being investigated—

24. Fernández, 156. He is referring to Deck, *The Second Wave*, xix.
25. Schreiter, "Contextualization in U.S. Hispanic Theology," 20.

especially, say, in the area of popular religiosity—were coming
from rural areas. The boundedness of the modern culture concept also makes it a more manageable category . . . One sees in
the newest generations of Hispanic intellectuals . . . used being
made of postmodern approaches.[26]

The Anthropological Impulse: A Theological Urgency

Latina/o theological anthropology examines traditional ways of defining
humanity and finds that anthropological definitions are possible without having to subscribe to the Anglo-European categories of thought.

We would like to consider a diverse community of theologians
that have contributed to the development of anthropological themes
relevant to Latina/o theologizing. A key discussion on this matter is
the anthropological survey by David Maldonado Jr. entitled "Doing
Theology and the Anthropological Questions."[27]

Maldonado starts his survey with an analysis of traditional ways
of doing theological anthropology. In his perception, the human entity,
traditionally speaking, is treated in isolation and much effort is made
trying to define what it means to be human in terms of body-soul categories. One of Maldonado's theses is that the individual is not understood
in isolation, disconnected from the human and social environment, but
rather as a social being in dynamic interrelationship with the human reality. So, in order to do anthropology it is necessary to take into account
the historical, cultural, and communal sources as well as the economic,
political, and social forces that shape and define human existence. In
this way, Maldonado positions his view within the framework of social
sciences in order to articulate theological anthropology.

As Maldonado presents his anthropological concepts, he deals
with three major Latina/o theologians who represent various traditions among the Latina/o community: the Mexican Catholic theologian
Virgilio Elizondo, the Cuban Protestant theologian Justo González, and
The Puerto Rican Pentecostal theologian Eldin Villafañe.

Through the work of Elizondo, Maldonado proceeds to describe
how Mexican-Americans are the product of of two major conquests:

---

26. Ibid., 30.

27. Maldonado, "Doing Theology and the Anthropological Questions," 98–111.

the Spanish-Catholic and the Nordic-Protestant.[28] In both cases, the conquest involved physical violence and socio-cultural and religious consequences for those who were the victims of the conquest. Elizondo's interpretation of the Latina/o experience, says Maldonado, points to God's choice of the lowly, the marginalized, and the rejected to bring the new reign. In Elizondo's own words, "what human beings rejected God chooses as his very own."[29] This is known in Elizondo's thought as the "Galilean principle." It is an interpretation given to the fact that God elected Galilean Jews (culturally marginalized and second class) to launch his kingdom on earth through the ministry of Jesus of Nazareth. This biblical antecedent becomes for Elizondo a hermeneutical tool to interpret Latino/a reality and to affirm that God, who knows their struggles and suffering, calls Latinos/as as partners in confronting the social structures and sinfulness of an oppressive society. In light of this, Maldonado highlights how theological anthropology, from a Latino/a perspective, is done within the confines of critical cultural analysis.

Maldonado also appeals to the thought of Justo González, a Cuban Protestant historian and theologian. According to González, to be Latina/o involves a concatenation of feelings: gratitude among the many political and economic refuges, and anger because Latinos/as live in a land defined as "not their land" where doors are closed. To be Latina/o is to be part of a minority group that is subject to injustice and marginalization. González himself, after biographical descriptions of his experience as a Protestant, says:

> [T]o be a Latina/o-Protestant means to be a pilgrim people on a journey toward the possible in which the spiritual is inseparable from the social. Latina/o Protestants are mañana (tomorrow) people. The people whose task is prophetic and whose hope is in the power and the promise of none other than the Almighty God.[30]

Maldonado wishes to underline the political dimension of Latino/a life as one of "exile" within the United States, thus illustrating how a political perception of the human entity is in tune with Latino/a theological anthropology.

28. Ibid., 102–3. Maldonado refers to Elizondo, *Galilean Journey*, 9–18.

29. Elizondo, *Galilean Journey*, 91.

30. Rodríguez and Martell-Otero, *Teología en Conjunto*, 105.

Maldonado's third expositor is the Pentecostal Puertorrican Eldin Villafañe, according to whom the reality of the Latinos in the United States is defined as the product of two types of factors and dynamics: cultural and sociodemographic. The former comes from three sources: Spanish, African, Amerindians. The latter is a group of factors that characterize the Latina/o culture: poverty, immigration, political marginality, educational limitations, urban concentrations, and general underclass status. Here, Villafañe, in a *Weberian* tone, attempts to describe the *homo Hispanicus* within the trinitarian formula of "culture, language, and race/ethnicity," thus providing Maldonado with a sociological profile for Latino/a theological anthropology.[31]

Maldonado finishes his essay by listing five factors that need to be considered in order to develop a holistic theological anthropology from the Latino/a perspective.

First, Maldonado lists *ethnic identity*, which refers to a sense of peoplehood: Latinos/as belong to the same population. Second, he describes *historical perspective*, which refers to the understanding of Latina/os as the human product of the historical conquest of Amerindian ancestors by the Spaniards. Third, *cultural roots* force Latina/os to understand that their roots include Spanish, Native Americans, and Africans (in some cases). The fourth factor, *social location and oppression*, highlights the reality that Latinos/as are among the poorest segments of the American society. Finally, the *community* factor points out the fact that Latino/a people can only be understood appropriately in relational terms. In other words, to be a Latina/o means participation in community.

After this review, Maldonado provides a definition of what is to be a Latina/o, anthropologically speaking:

> [To be a Latino/a is] to experience life as a member of the mestizo/mulato population,[32] which understands its birth in the context and outcome of the conquest and which has experienced oppression and colonialization throughout its history and continues today to identify with the poor and the oppressed.[33]

31. See Villafañe, *The Liberating Spirit*, 4 n11.

32. Here the term *mestizo* refers to a mixture of white European with Amerindian, while *mulato* refers to a mixture of black African with white Latin American. A clearer understanding of *mestizaje* will be offered in ch. 4.

33. Maldonado, "Doing Theology," 110.

In conclusion, Maldonado envisions theological anthropology in terms of cultural analysis, political perspective, and sociological views of what it means to be a human being in a Latino/a way. God's image in the human is assumed in these immanent anthropological categories, namely, cultural, political, and social.[34]

Popular Religion (Culture): A Theological Inevitability

According to Robert E. Wright *"popular religiosity* is that religiosity which is widely appropriated among the social group as a whole which is being considered—and thus necessarily among its common people or masses."[35] The notion that Latino/a culture (and evidently Latin American culture) was birthed with the Roman Catholic religious chromosome has been widely accepted among classical Latino/a theologians. Lately, however, theologians, anthropologists, and sociologists have taken a closer look into that religious chromosome and have learned that religiosity is indeed a vital part of these cultures, but that it is not merely a genetic religious factor; it is a sociocultural product as well. That is, religiosity among Latinos/as is an *organic* and *ongoing* social phenomena—a transnational reality.[36] In the thought of Goizueta, for instance, popular religiosity is a communitarian-social phenomena; it's the creation of the people.[37] Thus, any theological discourse attempting to speak of and for such a context will *inevitably* have to engage the religious practices and symbols of (this) culture. The generalization that Latinos/as are religious persons is indeed a thesis finely advanced by Roberto Goizueta in his work *Caminemos con Jesús*.[38]

The Catholic theologian Orlando Espín, however, is one who has more forcefully studied the realm of popular religiosity and who in-

34. It should be mentioned, however, that the three theologians, Elizondo, González, Villafañe, do recognize the transcendent character of God's image in the human subject. This was not very well reflected in Maldonado's exposition in view of underlining the cultural, political, and social aspect of doing anthropology from the Latino/a perspective.

35. See Wright, "If It's Official," 56.

36. We find a fine exposition on this matter in Vásquez and Marquardt, *Globalizing the Sacred*.

37. See especially Goizueta, *Caminemos con Jesús*, ch. 2.

38. Ibid., Goizueta argues that Roman Catholicism is the essential matrix of Latino/a culture(s).

deed gives basis for Goizueta's views. We will engage Espín's view of anthropology and popular culture as he exposes it in his essay *Grace and Humanness*.[39]

Espín begins his discussion on culture by establishing a relationship between God and humanity. That relationship assumes that God is a revealing God and that human beings exist as concrete and historical beings endowed by a particular cultural reality. That cultural reality is affected by God's revelation in a way that the human creature is able to perceive God's grace as revealed within such a reality, or to say it with Espín: "culture is a necessary prism through which we perceive God's grace and through which we respond to it."[40] Thus, context and culture, in Espín's opinion, are an intrinsic part of humanness. He declares,

> [W]e are not Catholics who happen to be Hispanic—we are Catholics in Hispanic way, and we cannot be in any other way. Our Hispanic culture thus makes us experience the grace of God in a specific fashion, a way that would not be available to us if we were not Latina/o.[41]

In this way Espín makes a case for a Latino/a theology—a theology with a particular hermeneutic, method and source—related to culture as its primal source.

Creation, for Espín, is the outpouring of God's grace and the first sacrament of God's love. Grace is "God-for-us." God, who is the ultimate source of humanness in the image of God, draws the path of what to be a human being means. That is,

> To be human is to be the image of love, of an eternally communitarian (that is trinitarian) God. And, as a consequence, one cannot claim to be truly human unless one is loving, and not just loving in an individual way also in a communitarian way (given the trinitarian reality of God).[42]

Because humanness comprises transhistorical and transcontextual elements (love and community) as well as historical and contextual elements (culture and geography) it can be sinful or deformed. Espín, develops the notion of humanization and dehumanization based on

39. See Espín, "Grace and Humanness," 133–64.
40. Ibid., 134
41. Ibid.
42. Ibid., 138.

the arguments he had previously presented. Historical processes that deprive persons of their freedom to give themselves in love and in community are dehumanizing. Similarly, historical processes that enable persons to become loving beings in community with others are humanizing. The purpose of human existence is then to become fully what the Creator intended us to be, namely, fully and authentically humans in his image. To live avoiding this reality or to passively tolerate dehumanizing historical processes is to live *becoming* what we are not, thus to live irresponsibly.[43]

Incarnation is important, for Espín, because it is the ultimate act of humanization through love. Christ, then personifies God's self in love (transcendence) and loving (immanence). "Our salvation is a wonderful by-product of the love of God shown in the incarnation and death and resurrection of the Son. We are saved because we are loved."[44]

So far, Espín has treated humanness theologically and biblically. Now, he will particularize these concepts in the cultural prism and give them material contend. For this task it is essential to lay down the following assumptions: One, we cannot be human and not be historical and geographical entities. Two, nothing human in Christianity is a-cultural. Three, our ways of being Christians will be necessarily cultural.

If these assumptions and theological notions are true then, says Espín:

> Deculturization, in the name of Christianity, would be dehumanizing and (as a consequence) sinful. To trample on Hispanic culture while pretending to evangelize is to impede the very experience of God that saves, because, as we have seen, the experience of grace can only be had in and through one's culture.[45]

In the same line of reasoning Espín claims that, "popular religiosity, has been, and still is, the least 'invaded' cultural creation of our peoples, and a locus for our most authentic self disclosure."[46] Popular religion, certainly, in Latin America and the U.S. Latina/o world is a major religious force. The creation of "informal" ways to God is not a new style of being a Christian. It is widely accepted the fact that the "official" Catholicism,

43. Ibid., 140.
44. Ibid., 142.
45. Ibid., 147.
46. Ibid., 148.

in Latin America for instance, is a minority while popular Catholicism is a majority. In this sense, Espín explains, "by this [popular] I do not merely mean that they are widespread. They are indeed. But these means are popular mainly because they literally come from the people themselves."[47]

Popular religiosity as a "privileged locus of Latina/o self disclosure and culture,"[48] Espín notices, help us discover what is to be human in the Latina/o sense. In his analysis, Espín observes that the ways Latinos/as relate to God are very similar to the typical father-child relationship. Motherhood is another crucial element of meaning among Latinos/as. The mother is the "loving center of the family . . . the conciliator,"[49] the materialization of sacrifice, the tolerant giver. Relatives, friends and neighbors are all part of an organic network of relationships that help overcome suffering and loneliness among Latinos/as. So Espín concludes that:

> Whatever else can be said about Hispanic understanding of what it means to be human, this necessarily must include the familial and communal dimensions. The individual is valued and important *because* he or she is a member of a family and of a community.[50]

In conclusion, Espín's theological anthropology makes an interesting case. On the one hand, Espín's anthropological perspective seems grounded in God's relationality with his human creatures. Such relationality is communal and based on *agape*. God as God is transcendence and mystery. On the other hand, God as creator is a relational being, whose relationality is experienced as immanence and cultural existence. From the human side, then, we have no way to know and relate to God other than by cultural and communal conducts. If this is true, Espín's view epitomizes theologizing with a *modern perception of culture* in mind.

Interestingly, Virgilio Elizondo, when using cultural analysis in theologizing, has noticed the risk of "confusing the cultural

47. Ibid., 152.
48. Ibid.
49. Ibid., 153.
50. Ibid., 154.

expressions of *our* faith with *the* faith."[51] Although Elizondo is referring to the tendency of dominant cultures/traditions when "evangelizing" non-dominant cultures, this warning can also be valid in order to notice a qualitative distinction between (cultural) Christian practices and *the* Christian faith. This observation assumes there is a boundary between God's self-revelation and the human (anthropology), a boundary that can only be overcome by God himself.

Lo Cotidiano and Popular-based Practices: A Theological Obligation

Roberto Goizueta capitalizes creatively on Espín's view of popular religiosity as the privileged space of God's revelation. We will not exhaust Goizueta's theological resources here. In following chapters we will revisit him in a more practical fashion. Here, we are interested in the sociocultural implications of Latino/a popular religiosity Goizueta develops in *Caminemos con Jesús.*[52]

Goizueta's contribution to Latino/a anthropology is geared more to the perception of the Mexican-American (Catholic) experience, although Goizueta himself is Cuban-American. His analysis reflects principles and characteristics that might be useful for theologizing. For Goizueta the human entity is relational and social in essence. As relational beings we are always connected to the *other* and only understood within a social and concrete (physical) context. Latino/a individuals, thinks Goizueta, are never "exclusively" a *he* or *she* but also a *nosotros* (us). Latinos/as (as any human being) are sacramental entities which mediate the divine and abstract into the concrete and cultural. Latinos/as, affirms Goizueta, are organically related to each other. Goizueta, via linguistic analysis, describes how every day (*lo contidiano*) language defines Latino/a life. For instance, when in Spanish one speaks of meeting with another person one uses the term *reunirnos*, which means "to re-encounter." This expresses, in Goizueta's perception, the essence of what Latinos/as are, namely, organically related and intrinsically united.

Another factor that Goizueta points to is that language for Latinos/as is more than mere expression of thoughts. Words carry

51. Elizondo, *Galilean Journey,* 47.

52. See Goizueta, *Caminemos con Jesús,* particularly 47–76, where he deals with his anthropology, and ch. 7, where he outlines his theology of accompaniment.

practical-personal meaning in the sense that words are acted upon in daily life. Our practice of life creates meaning, and that collective meaning affects our practice of life, understands Goizueta. That's why to say that Jesus is our *compañero* (companion) means more than "he can be or will be our partner." It means that he already is, in our most concrete experience, our partner. Meaning arises out of the community. A Latino/a is a being-in-community. Goizueta affirms that the Latino/a community is a sacramental community. So every time a Latino/a participates in the life of the community *meaning* arises and defines him/her. That is why popular religion, for Goizueta, is an authentic expression of the Latino/a community and therefore full of meaning and revelation.[53]

Goizueta, operating with a sacramental-theological anthropology and based on an analysis of *lo cotidiano* (everyday life), advances the thesis that *out of the concrete experience of popular Catholicism, as the privileged locus of God's revelation and thus of theological reflections, we are able [and obligated] to develop a theology "of" and "for" the U.S. Hispanic/Latina people, namely, a theology of accompaniment.* Goizueta's concept of *accompaniment* is central to the present work, thus a thorough understanding of this concept is provided in the final chapter. Suffice it here to say that *accompaniment* constitute a social paradigm of being-in-community that *reflects* Latino/a popular way of life and *refracts* native Latino/a paradigms for the church to *walk with* the Latino/a communities as true home, true family, and true worship community. God is conceived, within this cultural matrix, as a popular-concrete Jesus who ultimately represents the social-physical companion who takes the side of the suffering and oppressed and who in the journey will construct justice and well being "in" and "with" the Latino/a community. To walk with Latino/a communities, in this way, is for Goizueta the basis of a *theology of accompaniment* and therefore the basis of an ecclesial praxis that is a social obligation toward the community the church represents.

In sum, Goizueta embodies Espín's theological (cultural) anthropology in his concept of accompaniment and further develops an organic-sacramental anthropological vision where God is embodied and experienced in *physical sacramentality*. God is entirely embodied

---

53. Ibid., 18.

in popular faith. Participating in the popular faith community means, for Goizueta, knowing God in the concrete.[54]

Conclusions

So far we have offered three representative groups (*Founders, Builders, Shapers*) that in our judgment can help us see a continuum in the socio-theological development of Latino/a theologizing. We argued that *Founders* and *Builders* in particular were bound by the urgency of the Latino/a context to focus on anthropological themes to achieve a foundational understanding of cultural identity, namely, what it is to be Latino/a in the U.S. and reflect out of that experience.

The particular experience of being Latino/a within the U.S. context and *lo cotidiano* moved Latino/a theologizing to begin inquiring into the realm of popular culture and religion. Although most Latino/a theologians—from the Catholic and Protestant traditions—agree on the importance of popular religiosity in theological reflection, several influential theologians, particularly Roman Catholics, identified the religiosity of popular culture as the most appropriate cultural space for God's revelation and human self-disclosure. Popular religion and culture, in the Roman Catholic perspective, therefore, has taken a formal character and a primal role as *locus theologicus* of Latino/a theologizing.

Such is not the case of "formal" Latino/a theologizing from the Protestant perspective. As De La Torre and Aponte explain, there are several formative matrices that give shape to Latino/a Protestant religiosity including the sacramental-like role of Scripture, the marks of the Protestant reformation (*sola Scriptura, sola fide, sola gratia*), the domestic influence of the *spoken Word*, and more significantly the *formative role* of the Holy Spirit as the *originator* and *shaper* of faith and domestic religious practices.[55] On the other hand, we maintain that "informally" the great majority of Latino/a Protestant laity and clergy do accept popular religiosity (as a multi-matrix, complex, and fluid set of patterned religious practices) as sources for ministry, training of the laity, interpretation of Scripture, ethics, and, therefore, informal theology. One can verify this claim simply by surveying the issue of the popular bible institutes and their influence on Latino/a ministry. In these informal

54. See for instance ibid., 67–68, 196.
55. De La Torre and Aponte, *Introducing Latino/a Theologies*, 123.

ministry training centers the constituency of Latino/a Protestantism is taking shape. This underlines the fact that popular religiosity, in the Latino/a Protestant sense, has a *defining* yet *informal* character.

We concur with Robert Schreiter's comment that much of Latino/a theology has been developing out of a modern perception of culture.[56] We would add critically that this is true for the most part, particularly in the case of the *use* of the category of culture when theologizing. That is, the absence of the transcendent and a somehow *structural-mechanical* perception of culture undermines much of Latino/a theology. We acknowledge that much of Latin America has not experienced modernity in the same way Latinos/as have in the U.S., due in part to the imposing presence of Roman Catholicism and to the fact that modernity infiltrated Latin America in the form of a colonizing imperialistic enterprise.[57] An alternative trans-modern (indigenous but not anti-modern) cultural experience, in the form of popular religiosity that impacted the whole life of the Latin American person, was simultaneously developing. Even though this trans-modern experience has been the object of modern study (we share this view with Schreiter) it should be taken into account that this experience in itself surpasses modern anthropological and sociological methodology due to its *transcendent* and *indigenous* character. Thus Marcos Villamán's observation on this matter is worth quoting in full:

> Modernity, now entrenched in Latin American and Caribbean neoliberal modernizing projects, share the social space with popular cultures, even if modernity has established a relationship of submission on their part. Nevertheless, the *form(s) of the relationship* which these cultural products establish between themselves is *complex* [emphasis mine] . . . on one hand, popular cultures are penetrated by modernity and its own subjects are included on the modern horizon . . . On the other hand, however, we find expressions in the popular cultures which can be taken as demands of recognition of their own distinct being, and which firmly persist as irreducible differences.[58]

56. See p. 37–38 above.

57. See a brilliant discussion on this topic in Litonjua, "Pentecostalism in Latin America: Scrutinizing a Sing of the Times," 26–49.

58. See Villamán, "Church and Inculturation: Modernity and Culture in Latin America," 38.

It is precisely these *cultural forms* in complex relationship with other *forms* that share the same socio-historical context that characterizes the postmodern situation. It is little surprise that third world theologies, including Latino/a theology, find themselves in a *privileged position* with regard to expressing their missiology and ecclesiology theologically in a postmodern environment. It is certain that Latino/a theologizing must deal with the postmodern context (the current context of urban *latinidad*), hopefully with inspiring biblical narratives, original communal practices, and a transformative language.

Because Latino/a theologizing has operated with a *modern* understanding of culture, the discourse has been forced to speak within the confines of *modern cultural anthropology*, thus leaving the *historical transcendent Spirit of God* out of the picture or subdued to *historical-immanent* categories of thought and practice. Because of this fact and acknowledging the indubitable reality of our *new situation*—the postmodern context—we turn now to explore some perceptions and challenges this *new context* brings to Latino/a theologizing.

Cultural Postmodern Perceptions and Challenges

The distinctiveness among people and communities is at the center of what we call culture. Cultural perceptions have connected from the beginning to anthropological views—although as a science, anthropology is a daughter of modernity. As anthropological perceptions have changed in dominant societies so has the understanding of culture.[59] Thus, defining culture is a complex matter and it will not satisfy every reader, for inevitably every reader is an interpreter of culture.

We render culture as *that which in practice associates us and disso-ciates us from peoples and communities making possible the transmission of forms of life from generation to generation.* We do not mean traits

---

59. Tanner sees, for instance, that postmodernity has modified the anthropological notion of culture. See Tanner, *Theories of Culture*, x. For pre-modern and modern times, a similar analogy can be maintained. As a matter of fact, Ancient Greek philosophy dominated Western thought and theology for centuries before critical thinking—particularly Cartesian and that of Spinoza—doubted the epistemological foundations of such ideas concerning the perception of what it means to be a human being. In modern times, Natural Science, along with the Skeptics, affected dramatically the perception of the human and some argue eclipsed the true perception of what it means to be human. This claim is made by the Greek Orthodox theologian Philip Sherrad in his anthropological treatise *The Eclipse of Man and Nature*.

linked to biology, physiognomy, geography or merely an ideology or value or belief save it is a "practiced ideology" or a "practiced value" or a "practiced-belief" of a community in a given social context. *Why* do we associate with others and *to what end?* This is precisely what entertains cultural-related studies and other academic disciplines that have joined the discussion of culture.[60] Our interest in this section, however, is not the elaboration of scientific social theory but to attain a functional understanding of how can culture be used by theological inquiry as *the most primal and formative-socializing matrix* where by the propagation of religious forms of life is achieved. In this sense, we accept the Latino/a theological premise that culture is an essential *loci of human and divine praxis* and that such a *loci* is essential in the theological process. What we need to discern, however, is how culture is to be perceived as a category able to embrace both the transcendence of God's Spirit and the complexity and inextricable diversity of today's peoples' identities. In other words, in the present work we intend not to host an innocent reading of culture, one assuming that our modern anthropological and theological tools can decipher and objectively (or subjectively) interpret culture or cultural practices or the like as reflecting God's activity and character, or even human essence and purpose, without conditions.

With this understanding in mind, we are to examine three perceptions and challenges that highlight the limitations of theologizing with a modern approach, and simultaneously, we will entertain postmodern cultural perceptions.

Culture and Its Political Implications

Some cultural experts argue that in pre-modern times religion was for the most part coexisting with culture, while in modern societies, especially in the West, a more utilitarian idea of culture developed as deinstitutionalization took place and societies became more and more modernized and secularized (e.g., separation of church and state). This utilitarian concept is well illustrated in societies such as England. According to Masuzawa, a dramatic shift in the meaning of culture occured in the nineteenth century due in part to factors such as industrialization, democracy and social class struggle. Culture evolved from a "process of human training" toward a concept in itself referring to

60. Tanner, *Theories of Culture*, 3.

a state to of the mind, intellectual development within society, artistic achievement, and so on.[61]

Put simply, culture became a principle of edification of the individual and rectification of the community in many of the influential societies of Europe and North America. Soon enough, the West imagined itself as the supreme cultural standard with the duty of civilizing the rest of the world. At this point, culture had become a powerful political tool in modern society. The notion of a national culture spirit as well as the idea of the state as the agent of human perfection in an organic society have co-constructed governmental bodies, delineated the private sector, and even re-defined the role of religion in modern societies. So, Masuzawa concludes that religion's role as the civilizing agent of society has been severely altered giving way to the state as the new edifying social organ.[62] Consequently, as history attests, the idea of culture has been used by dominant societies and industries as a colonizing and commercializing artifact. Herbert and Williams have contributed,[63] observes Masuzawa, to the idea that culture has not been merely "an idea," so to speak, but "an argument, a moral persuasion" at the disposal of political and economic structures in the process of colonizing sub-powers.[64]

Similarly, we see Robert Schreiter's theological finger pointing to the problem of globalization and its *identity politics*.[65] On the one hand, globalization paints a "more uniform world," but on the other hand, "foments fragmentation and resistance" at the local level.[66] One of the ways fragmentation takes place at the local level, according to Schreiter, is by the "reassertion of local identities."[67] However, the reassertion of identities within a postmodern context is extremely complex since such a context promotes "the absence of a master narrative" and "absolutizes

61. See the discussion on culture in Masuzawa, "Culture," 70–93.

62. Ibid., 72–77.

63. Raymond William and Christopher Herbert are important literary scholars in the line of "cultural representation." Here, Masuzawa refers to Herbert, *Culture and Anomie*, and William, *Culture and Society*.

64. Masuzawa, "Culture," 90.

65. Schreiter, "Contextualization in U.S. Hispanic Theology," 27–29.

66. Ibid., 27.

67. Ibid., 28.

the difference" among each culture and community.[68] This postmodern political phenomenon ends up generating chaos with regard to communication among different cultures and communities.

In conclusion, Masuzawa, on the one hand, points to the fact that culture has not been utilized innocently within the academic, social, and political arena. The modern use of cultural discourse entails a colonizing gene. Though Latino/a theologizing has been conscious of this fact and critical about colonizing discourses, a modern perception of culture is always at risk of falling into colonizing-colonized categories.[69] On the other hand, Schreiter confronts us with the imminent reality of *identity politics* crisis, particularly in the urban contexts of the United States. Latino/a theologizing is not to simply deny such a reality or adopt a tribal position about it, for our communities are dealing with the chaotic and critical "concrete" situation of having to live in multiple-identity settings.[70] We need, therefore, a cultural perspective that is post-colonial in scope. In this sense, we pair with Justo González who calls for a "metamodern view," which is essentially "post-colonial," as an alternative to that kind of postmodern view which tends to be deconstructionist about any common matrix of identity (e.g., Bible) making almost impossible the existence of specific ethnicities, cultures or people.[71]

Culture and Its Theological Implications

Kathryn Tanner offers a provocative cultural review geared toward a postmodern use of culture when elaborating theological discourse. When surveying the historical development of the concept of culture in Europe, she notices that in pre-modern times there seems to be a *singular* understanding of culture in contrast to a *plural* understanding

---

68. Ibid.

69. In this particular regard, the critique of Giacomo Cassese on the cultural approach of U.S. Latino/a theology seems appropriate. That is, there is a risk of innocently using (modern) cultural analysis—one that assumes a level of homogeneity, such as not acknowledging heterogeneity in religiosity or social class—when theologizing and not noticing the colonizing ideology hidden in modern cultural discourse. See Cassese, "De la Iglesia y el Estado Omnipotente," 115–16.

70. A good source that compiles essays on such a reality is Delgado and Stefancic, eds., *The Latino/a Condition.*

71. González, "Metamodern Alieans in Postmodern Jerusalem," 347–50.

of culture represented in modern societies and a more *hybrid* perception found in postmodern settings.[72]

With regard to the elaboration of theological discourses from a modern perspective, Tanner becomes very suspicious. The modern approaches toward culture, for Tanner, are misleading and thus require reconstruction.[73] In reality, as modern anthropologists believe, cultures are social wholes, but contrary to their views these are "contradictory and internally fissured wholes" due to the imminent social flux. Therefore, cultural relations are somehow chaotic, disorganized, and far form ascertained by all. "Consensus" within the new postmodern paradigm is understood more likely as an ongoing process or the result of "social engagement" more than "social agreement." In Tanner's words,

> [C]ulture brings people together as a common focus for engagement … [they] are bound together by a common attachment to or investment in such [any given] cultural items, and not necessarily by any common understanding of what they mean.[74]

The postmodern anthropologist's task, in short, revolves around pointing out the complexity and diversity within any given culture, focusing on alternative ways of social engagements, promoting self-criticism, resisting any definition of culture as a homogeneous and consistent form of life, and re-orienting the tendency of cultural inter-differentiation toward cultural intra-differentiation.[75] Similarly, the postmodern theologian is to elaborate his/her theology within this diverse and complex context avoiding any type of *dogmatocentrism*, admitting the plurality and fluidity of its social context when constructing theological discourse which, as culture, is far from being a homogeneous and consistent reality. Indeed, theology is better conceived by Tanner as part of culture, as a form of cultural activity.[76] The starting point of such theologizing

72. For a detailed account of how the understanding of culture has progressed from pre-modern times within Euro-American dominated contexts, see Tanner, *Theories of Culture*, 4–37.

73. Tanner understands these approaches to be: 1) inattention to historical process, 2) cultures are internally consistent wholes, 3) cultures are build on consensus or social agreement, 4) cultures are view as a principle of social order, 5) cultures are virtually stable wholes in themselves, and 6) cultures are self-contained units. Ibid., 40–56.

74. Ibid., 57.

75. Ibid., 58.

76. Ibid., 66.

(cultural activity) is always the concrete situation of real life. Like the anthropologist, the theologian is responsible to re-interpret the cultural materials in light of the context and in relationship with the Christian community.

There are some significant challenges that this postmodern understanding of culture presents to Christian theology and the Christian community. Tanner points to issues pertaining to Christian identity, Christian consensus, and Christian witness. For instance, Tanner observes that Christian identity should not be based on cultural/social/religious differentiation—what makes us different from non Christian people—for the boundaries of such a distinctiveness are unclear. Identity, for Tanner, is essentially *relational*.[77] Identity constructs itself in the process of engagement and exchange within a culture. It follows that experiences and concrete situations are factors when building one's own identity and defining one's own boundaries within a given culture. Thus, boundaries are not fixed structures; they can fluctuate and so can identities. Consequently, Christian social practices, for instance, are bound to context and subject to being modified according to one's identity within that particular context.

But how is one to be a distinctive Christian person in a non-Christian society? Tanner responds, "a Christian way of life is essentially parasitic; it has to establish relations with other ways of life, it has to take from them, in order to be one itself."[78] She insists that Christians are largely identified by their shared investigative foci and concerns. They may not agree on the meaning of the foci or have the same convictions about the concerns, but the mutuality distinguishes Christians in the larger culture.[79]

Similarly Christian consensus, in Tanner's view, is not achieved by adding followers to our differentiated perception of a subject. Consensus is not necessarily based on social agreement but *on social engagement*. Ongoing disagreements, for Tanner, can be overcome when we are "encouraged to make of our Christian social practices a genuine

---

77. Ibid., 108–19.
78. Ibid., 113.
79. Ibid., 124–25.

community of argument, one marked by mutual hearing and criticism ..., by a common commitment to mutual correction and uplift."[80]

Following Tanner's logic then, Christian witnessing—the public testimony of our faith to others—is not based primarily on *what* makes us different from others or that we need to share, but on *how* we share what we believe. Tanner asserts, "The difference between Christian and non-Christian practices is not a matter of direct contrast ... of Christian affirmations or terms that are simply absent from non-Christian outlooks." It is rather a matter of "renunciation to prior practices" and the appropriation of one's life in "a radically different form."[81] Indeed, this is the meaning of Christianity as a second birth, argues Tanner. It is then how we practice the same life in a radically different way the strongest transformational argument when witnessing to others because it is based on community and practiced belief.

In conclusion, Tanner has highlighted significant cultural challenges that theology and the Christian community, in general, are facing within the postmodern context. Christian identity, consensus, and witnessing, as articulated by Tanner, are essentially socio-religious constructs. In this fluctuating cultural matrix, cultural items such as social boundaries, social plurality, and the transmission of belief are based on relationality instead of rationality; therefore, they can be negotiated. What gives identity to a group, in Tanner's view, challenges in a direct way the conception that, for instance, Latino/a "identity" is based on a "universal/consistent matrix," (e.g., culture, language, religion, ethnicity). Latino/a cultural identity, following Tanner's logic, is socially and relationally constructed. The current context, cultural convenience, and the social practices of people—who come together in the interest of commonality as they participate in the *imagined community* called Latino/a—seem for Tanner the formative elements of such identity. It should be noticed that Harold Recinos, in a Latino/a fashion, has paired with Tanner's logic by arguing that, in an urban context cultural pluralism should be a goal, but the goal will present a challenge to the church. The church, to thrive and exercise prophetic witnessing in such a context, will have to acquire cross-cultural competence in order to evangelize its immediate context (e.g., American culture) by means of

80. Ibid., 123.
81. Ibid., 113.

ecclesial practices that would bring about reconciliation, justice, and peace.[82]

We perceive also in Tanner's view the lack of an explicit recognition of the transcendent element (Spirit of God) in the process of identity formation. Although, she seems to regard the Spirit as a "free agent" in the process of Christian relationality, who blows according to its own will (not ours).[83] However, Tanner's view counts on human cultural capacity and creativity (relationality) as the formative factors for identity formation, leaving unsolved and open the issue of the role of the Spirit of God in the identity-making process of the Christian community.

Culture and the Challenge of the Transmission of Belief

Kathryn Tanner has provided a critical framework of theological analysis by which we can revise the whole theologizing enterprise in light of emerging cultural categories. Still, an important matter requires further illustration: how is the transmission of belief achieved from the Christian community to the non-Christian community? In other words, if theology is a form of cultural activity—a self-transmissible, self-making of cultural matter mediated by relationality—and if, within the current cultural matrix, identities are negotiated, social boundaries fluctuate, and *form* reigns over *content*; and if all these items are social constructs, then how do we make Christian culture? This very complex process is what we will attempt to illustrate through the thought of the French philosopher and social scientist Régis Debray, director of the European Institute of the History and Science of Religion at the Ecole practique des haustes études.

For Debray *mediology* (the art of transmission) emerges as the most appropriate way to understanding, classifying, and anticipating the process of cultural production. Mediology is at the same time method and object of study dealing with the matter of culture and its propagation in time and space. Mediology focuses strictly on the transmission process. It possesses a "material, diachronic, and political" dimension.[84]

In its material form, transmission is simply "making known, making familiar" the *codes of*, for instance, ideas and beliefs. It is a *link* be-

---

82. See Recinos, *Good News from the Barrio*, esp. ch. 5.

83. Tanner, *Theories of Culture*, 119.

84. Debray, *Transmitting Culture*, 1.

tween the material and immaterial realms. Thus, icons, organizations, rituals, and practices are materializations of meaning, as they reflect forms of life. One could also see traditions such as Islam, Christianity, or military organizations, as embodiments of ideas with self-inventing attributes: "No tradition has come about without being an invention or recirculation of expressive marks and gestures. No movement of ideas has occurred that did not imply the corresponding movement of human bodies...."[85]

A distinctive feature of the process of transmission, as contrasted with communication, is that transmission's medium of propagation is space rather than time. In other words, "transmission has a geography."[86] Debray observes that human beings because of their individuation and temporality communicate within a dialogical matrix and only rarely transmit lasting meaning. Organizations, rituals, practices, cultures, on the other hand, are spatial complexes that contain and conduct meaning—a lasting meaning capable of perpetuating over time. This takes us to transmission's political dimension, according to Debray.

Transmission, for Debray, points to "duty, mission, obligation, in a word, culture."[87] Transmission, having overcome the biological limitation, is capable of enduring the propagation of meaning. In this sense, transmission is not socially-based but political in essence: "as do all functions serving to transmute an undifferentiated mass into an organized whole . . . it is one of the stakes of civilization."[88] In sum, *culture* is a system of transmission of meaning—a collective framework for the process of civilizing and transforming life.

What then are the dynamics of cultural transmission according to Debray? Since the essence of culture is transmissibility, culture obeys principles or requires a discipline. Also *the matter* worth transmitting is very important as it is the medium or territory through which culture will become relevant and will perpetuate.

Debray's mechanics accept no easy categorization.[89] He describes better what he is not referring to (e.g., sociology, religion, communica-

85. Ibid., 2.

86. Ibid., 4.

87. Ibid., 5.

88. Ibid., 6.

89. An evolutionary theory of cultural transmission could be one way to describe Debray's mechanics.

tion, anthropology) than what he is advocating. Debray's interest rests on a discipline that "administers signs and images" and deals with its "tangible" effects on human bodies.[90] In Debray's own words:

> [A] discipline whose object is the relations between the superior social functions of art, religion, and ideology and the sociotechnical structures of transmission, in other words, ipso facto, *the way and means of cultural symbols' efficacy*.[91]

When dealing with *that matter which is to be transmitted*—as well as the *medium* of propagation—Debray elaborates creatively. Although for Debray the *medium* is not meaning (the message) in itself, nevertheless it is meaningful. Without a *medium* there is no clear and lasting meaning.

There is an inner logic in the process of perpetuating meaning that Debray names "organized matter and materialized organization."[92] This perhaps is the key to understanding Debray's view of cultural transmission. Debray focuses on finding out "how explicit symbolic systems are perpetuated in religions, ideologies, doctrines, and artistic productions." In more concrete terms: "how is it that," for instance, "two thousand years after Jesus, there still subsists something like Christianity in the Western world?"[93] Debray proposes an integrated model that relates *matter and organization* or *message and community*. Debray's eludes any formal attempt to explain causality (message precedes community vis-à-vis) and concentrates on instrumentality (mediology), that is, the fact that meaning requires community to perpetuate. To say it differently, there is not historical succession without a corporate body that exteriorizes (carries) meaning. The phenomenology of cultural transmission is complex and symbiotic. Debray sees culture in a symbiotic way: *cultura culturata and cultura culturans*. The idea of a dialectic mode of cultural production is at stake: one aspect of making culture refers to the *passive, constant, predictable, material—social/civic* structures that form the tissue of cultural life. Debray describes it with the notion of *cultura culturata*. The (other)coexisting aspect of cultural transmission has to do with an *active, innovative, transcending, becoming*, fluidity of

90. Ibid., 9.
91. Ibid., 10.
92. Ibid., 10.
93. Ibid., 9.

meaning. Debray describes it with the concept of *cultura culturans*.[94] This symbiotic operation of cultural transmission makes possible, for Debray, the perpetuation of meaning. In simple terms, *organized matter* is the message that abides in a structural form of life (e.g., a community). Community, on the other hand, is a historical, or in the words of Debray, essentially *materialized organization* (embodied message). Debray points to the fact that, "the message that does not find an institutional housing will go up in smoke or be drained off as so much background noise by the ambient environment of cultural life."[95] Again, the message and the community are not two disconnected, autonomous elements in the process of transmission, they are symbiotic modes of meaning existing in space and perpetuating over time. Debray elaborates:

> The art of transmission, or making culture, consists of adding a strategy to a logistics, a praxis to a techne, or establishing an institutional home and engineering a lexicon of signs and symbols. What persists over time is the art of composition; the proportion of elements varies.[96]

All this suggests, that community or social interaction forms the basis of the geography of culture. To illustrate, Debray presents us with the case of Christianity. Christianity, Debrays notices, constitutes a new ecclesiastical territory.[97] That "Christ died and resurrected" is the "causal argument" for the existence of Christianity. Yet what is more relevant, for Debray as a mediologist, is the fact that such a belief became a historical stimulus and "was objectified, formulated, and reformulated by a church that learned to assure its perpetuation across the centuries, down to our own."[98] Debray continues, "It is irrelevant to mediology whether Jesus of Nazareth was raised from the dead on the third day; the central question is to know *how* the tradition that established him was elaborated and carried on."[99] We hear in Debray, the postmodern

---

94. The symbiotics of culture is perhaps an echo of Benedict de Spinoza's view of nature—*natura naturata and natura naturans*. Once Spinoza's view is understood, Debray's counterpart concept is more intelligible. See Spinoza, *Ethics*.

95. Debray, *Transmitting Culture*, 11.

96. Ibid., 13.

97. Ibid., 15.

98. Ibid., 18–20.

99. Ibid., 9, emphasis added.

emphasis in the *how*, in the instrumentality of social embodied practices, in the mediology of Tanner's community of argument.

The essence of culture for Debray is transmission. It was because beliefs were appropriated "in and as" community that Christianity has been able to propagate as a cultural reality, according to the logic of Debray. In a postmodern tone Debray declares, "a mediological approach would do well to renounce the idealist's illusion that our culture is founded on a few simple formulations or messages that brought about its present state."[100] In the same line of thought, Debray advises, "if you wish to understand a theology, examine its corresponding ecclesiology: you will pass from the form to the formative matrix."[101] So using mediology, Debray illustrates the relevance of Tanner's community of argument in relation, for instance, to Christian witnessing. Christian witnessing, following Debray's logic, means transmitting culture within culture as an embodied message.

In conclusion, Debray has pointed to transmissibility and embodiment as the key elements of culture. For Debray, the message or *organized matter* (e.g., doctrine, interpretation, meaning) constitute the *form,* but the community itself or *materialized organization* is the formative matrix in cultural production. Both form a symbiosis out of which cultural forms of life emerge. Culture subsists and is transmitted based on this symbiotic dynamism. In Debray's view, for instance, *latinidad* and the *Latino/a community* is to emerge out of this symbiosis. That is, a community is "a Latino/a community" insofar it embodies *latinidad* and perpetuates itself as *materialized organization*, embodiment. In this sense, common historical events, shared context, similarity of experience (e.g., oppression and marginalization) constitute a *formative matrix* insofar as these are *mediated through* social engagement and become *materialized organization* or embodiment. Should these elements fluctuate, the culture that mediates them will also change accordingly.

Debray, given his mediologist perspective on culture, deems transcendent elements only as causal arguments. In this sense, Debray does not deny that the Holy Spirit, for instance, has a role in Christian cultural production. However, should not the community embody the experience of the Spirit, its relevance disappears.

100. Ibid., 19.
101. Ibid., 20.

Conclusion

So far, we have presented several challenges to Latino/a theologizing in the matters of a modern perception of culture. Doing theology with a modern understanding of culture takes the risk of limiting theological discourse to colonial-colonized cultural language, thus becoming a political casualty of the kind of discourse Latino/a theology seeks to overcome. We call, therefore, for a post-colonial, postliberal, postmodern view of culture that does not dis-empower minority groups and that allows for the empowering *historical transcendent* Spirit of Christ.

Doing theology from a modern perspective lacks anthropological language and tools to see culture in fluid and heterogeneous terms. This can be detrimental to Latino/a theologizing for such theological activity alleges to be *descriptive* and *representational* of the Latino/a people, a people possessing multiple matrixes of identities. So, Tanner points to culture as *relationality,* instead of *rationality,* to explain social boundaries, social plurality, and Christian identity. We call, therefore, for a *relational* perception of culture that allows for heterogeneity and for a *Spirit-to-human spirit* type of relationality.

Finally, doing theology with a modern understanding of culture limits our perception on how culture is produced and transmitted, for it assumes a universal-unchanging core underlying culture. Debray has advanced the claim that culture is based on *embodiment* and *transmissibility.* As such, culture is *transmission* of an *embodied* message. Herein, culture is not a static/passive category of epistemology or ontology. Culture is a dynamic-evolving symbiosis of message and community with the task of perpetuating meaning. We call, therefore, for a perception of culture that sees the Christian community as the embodied message of Jesus Christ, that is, the *community of the Spirit* with the mission of perpetuating meaningful life (practices) within the geography of non-Christian culture. In such a view, the Spirit is present not only as "a causal argument" but as a *cultural subject* who is also *an authoring* agent of Christian experience.

Toward a Postmodern *Spirit-friendly* Cultural Paradigm

The term postmodern carries within a connotation of tragedy and hope, confusion and validity, annihilation and resurgence. Some have even put a date on the birth of postmodernism. "It was born," argues

Stanley Grenz, "in St. Louis Missouri on July 15 of 1972, at 3:32 P.M.," when the government agreed to demolish the Pruitt-Igoe housing project, a construction intended to produce the perfect society aimed by the state-to-the-art modern technology. The government gave up when "unimpressed inhabitants vandalized the building."[102]

So it seems that postmodernism (as an ideological perception) marks the end of modernity and the beginning of a new and yet indefinable epoch. On the one hand, *postmodernism*—a relativistic, affectionistic, and pragmatic view of reality—represents a way of perceiving truth while creating meaning and practices.[103] On the other hand, *postmodernity*—a time of cultural shift and radical pluralism—describes a *heterotopian-pluricentered* life in a global society. Culturally speaking, it describes life as fiction, and fiction as life.[104] The following quote might illustrate this new concept:

> The disappearing of the ego [is] the victory sign of postmodernism . . . The self transformed into an empty screen of an exhausted, but hypertechnical culture. . . .[105]

In this context of *disappearing of the ego* and *hypertechnical culture*, we are to speak of God and Spirit in a way that *make sense* communally, theologically, and spiritually.

Alex García-Rivera's Approach to Postmodernism[106]

Speaking of God (theology) is an *a posteriori* event to that of experience, so argue liberation and Latino/a theologians. Postmodern approaches, however, seem to suggest that there is no *a priori* or *a posteriori* but there is only experience before, between, and beyond subjective reality. Hence, some view postmodernity as a *turning away* from individual-subjectivism *toward* experience itself as the realm of perpetual mediation.[107]

102. Grenz, *A Primer on Postmodernism*, 11.

103. See Ibid., ch. 2.

104. Ibid.

105. Kroker, Kroker, and Cook, "Panic Alphabet," 16.

106. Alejandro "Alex" García-Rivera teaches systematic theology at the Jesuit School of Theology at Berkeley. One of García-Rivera's most important theological contributions is *The Community of the Beautiful*, where he further develops his theological aesthetics.

107. García-Rivera refers here to Don Gelpi, *The Turn to Experience in Contemporary*

While liberation methodologies assume, argues Alex García-Rivera, that experience has an *author* (human subject) and that experience can be *read* (interpreted), postmodern approaches assert experience is *all there is*.[108] Experience, in a postmodern perspective, has no one-author; it expresses itself in terms of mediation, of a zigzag repeating of subjective interactions that take the subjects from one experience to the next. Human experience, in itself, cannot be interpreted as objective *matter* (a modern notion) but it can be perceived or "seen" in "otherness" or "alterity" or *différance*.[109] In this sense, experience encompasses a complex interaction of multiple epistemic matrices. García-Rivera suggests that in liberation theological discourse the concept of the poor as an objective experiential category (the different other) and the utopian idea of human emancipation, creates an inner tension yet unsolved in liberation discourse.[110] The fact that liberation theology has identified the poor as the "different other" and "authors of their own history," allows for the postmodern attack on the subject, so García-Rivera note "how liberation theology is able to assert that, at once, human experience has an author yet, above all, is to be seen."[111]

The problematic is resumed in the fact that postmodern language, as we have said, disregards the possibility of objective knowledge or that human experience has an identifiable-beyond-experience author. Essentialy, explains García-Rivera, postmodern language functions within a Saussurean-like *dyadic sign system*.[112] In such a linguistic system, the middle relationship between the subjects disappears leaving only an "inter-subjective construction" or *différance* (inter-subjective distinctiveness).[113] García-Rivera, however, notices that this kind of linguistic analysis, has a *blind spot* in that it "assume[s] without questioning that the intersubjective relationship, i.e., the relation of difference, is purely arbitrary . . . As such, postmodernism, while taking

---

Theology. See García-Rivera, "Creator of the Visible and the Invisible," 51.

108. García-Rivera, "Creator of the Visible and the Invisible," 43.

109. García-Rivera interacts here with Jacques Derrida, "Structure, Sign, and Play," and Leonard Lawlor, *Imagination and Chance*.

110. García-Rivera, "Creator of the Visible and the Invisible," 43.

111. Ibid.

112. Ibid., 51.

113. Ibid.

experience seriously, does not do the same for reality."[114] Under these conditions, theologizing in a way that promotes belief and salvation is virtually impossible, for there is no ground for such a reality. In the same vein, David Bentley Hart alleges that the problem of postmodernism is a *modern one*. That is, leading postmodern theorists continue to carry on vestiges of modern presuppositions. Hart explains:

> Where the discourse of fashionable postmodernism should become distasteful to theological reflection, in fact, is not in its alleged "relativism" or "skepticism," but in its failure sufficiently to free itself from the myths of modernity . . . a dogmatic metanarrative of its own [that there is no metanarratives].[115]

García-Rivera, *free* from this type of myth, offers an alternative approach that accepts the postmodern view of intersubjective relationality but that does not lose the *sense of reality*. García-Rivera, then, elaborates a *triadic sign approach*.[116]

Assisted by the anthropological-philosophical views of the American philosopher, Charles Peirce, and the insights of the Iberian Dominican philosopher, John Pointsot, García-Rivera constructs a postmodern perception that can be called *Spirit-friendly*. Put shortly, in the process of intersubjective relationality a third factor enters into play: the intersection of these intersubjective relationships by which they cannot only be "seen" but also "read," (just like in thermometers, where the intensity of heat is readable at a particular variation point).[117] This third factor is to function as a *sign* or a *referral* (renvoi) traveling along with the subjects and *différance* in a given experience. García-Rivera attempts an illustration to explain his view:

> Postmodern experience may, for example, merely associate one ant with another ant and another, i.e., the otherness of the difference between the ants [*différance*], as the experience of an army of ants. The story, however, lies not so much in the experience of an army of ants but in the difference between an army in *rout* or an army in *march*.[118]

114. Ibid., 52.

115. Hart, *The Beauty of the Infinity*, 6. Here Hart is elaborating on Lyotard's assessment of postmodernism as articulated in *The Postmodern Condition*.

116. García-Rivera, "Creator of the Visible and the Invisible."

117. Ibid., 52–55.

118. Ibid., 54.

This example is illuminating. While *différance* points merely to a distinctiveness of the interaction between subjects, *renvoi* points to an *intersection* of the "trajectories" or "stories" of those subjects in relationship. *Renvoi* functions, then, as a *referral*, a *sign* pointing to something other than the intersubjective *différance*.[119]

In this way, García-Rivera's approach accepts the postmodern conception of *différance* as the perpetual commuting of subjects within which a distinctiveness is perceivable in their intersubjectivity. As such, no objective knowledge is possible. However, there is a third factor, namely *renvoi*, which is the intersection of the stories of these intersubjective relationships. This intersection functions as a sign or *referral* pointing to something other than *différance*. While we cannot "read" (interpret) the subjects interrelationality, we can "read" (understand) their stories or trajectories.

Within this complex paradigm, García-Rivera finds that it is possible to speak of God as the *creator of the visible and the invisible*. For such a task, García-Rivera points to a "theology of creation" as the basis of theologizing within a postmodern context. A theology of creation, for this matter, tells the story of God (the Big Story) and creation. Thus, García-Rivera uses the faith statement: "I believe in God, Maker of all things, visible and the invisible," as the centric theme of his view. García-Rivera understands that this statement suggests "there is a difference between the *created* invisible and the *uncreated* invisible," giving the *created* invisible a middle place between the *uncreated* invisible (God) and the *created* visible (human beings).[120] According to García-Rivera, this middle (*created invisible*) place is a juncture or intersection, where the human subject can exercise belief, repentance, and create religious meaning. In simple terms, this space is where we can turn toward God "making visible the invisible."[121]

Following García-Rivera's logic, we suggest that what he calls the "*created* invisible" refers to the intersection of the Spirit of God (*uncreated* invisible) with humanity (*created* visible)—a space which is spiritually fecund. Furthermore, we suggest that such a *created* invisible reality is to be understood as the *experience of the Spirit*. We are referring to an

119. Ibid., 53.
120. Ibid., 54.
121. Ibid., 38.

intersubjective experience where the human subject encounters the *historical transcendent Spirit* as a *subject* and *narrator* or *referral* of God's Big story. In this sense, the *created* invisible refers to the *realm of the experience of the Spirit.* In such a realm there is the possibility of turning toward God, of interpreting God's story as witnessed by Scriptures, of becoming new creation in Jesus Christ, and of imagining transformative cultural practices that are to be *made visible* by the Christian community (the *created* visible culture of the Spirit).

Culture as Embodiment, Relationality, and Transmissibility: Dyrness's Theology of Creation and Culture

We concur with García-Rivera in the fact that a theology of creation is the best complement toward a postmodern perspective of culture that is *Spirit-friendly.* In a sense, William Dyrness argues correspondingly.

Dyrness understands that God is involved in creation in action and presence.[122] Humanity is, then, a sign of God's involvement with creation. Human beings are necessarily cultural for we are "embodied social creatures."[123] Accordingly, culture results out of human relationality with creation, thus "culture is what we make of creation."[124] Naturally, then, when we participate in the culture-making process we encounter or engage with God. Again, God is actively involved in creation as a sustainer and renewer.

Interestingly, Dyrness echoes our perspective of culture as embodiment, relationality, and transmissibility. In this sense, Dyrness represents a theological partner, from a Reformed tradition and a theology of creation perspective, that further supports our view of culture. The functional dimension of culture is depicted by Dyrness in a threefold way: culture is *patterned relationships, agency,* and *sanctuary (embodiment).*[125] Dyrness's threefold modality can be said to correspond to our three conceptual developments: embodiment (Debray), relationality (Tanner), and transmissibility (Debray). What is more significant, however, is that Dyrness sees the Holy Spirit as a liberating cultural subject who creates "unheard of options" within culture. The Holy Spirit is

122. See Dyrness, *The Earth Is God's,* ch. 3.
123. Ibid., 84.
124. Ibid., 58.
125. Ibid., 67–81.

God's transformational agent within creation (thus culture), with the task of creating "unheard of possibilities," which ultimately will glorify God.[126] In the same way, the Word of God functions as a "dynamic factor in cultural change," serving as a cultural resource for hearing God's good news, for inhabiting God's promises, for discerning God's will, and for imagining transformative cultural practices.[127]

Finally, the church is God's continuing presence in creation as the body of Christ. For Dyrness, "the Holy Spirit has ... been poured out to invade our social beings (including, potentially, all our cultural spaces) in order to bring all this to perfection," and since the Christian community is to respond to God's involvement in creation by *creating culture*, then the church, we suggest, is the *created* visible-culture of the Spirit within the *created* visible creation.[128] As such, the Christian community represents the embodied message of Jesus Christ with the mission of perpetuating meaningful life through cultural practices within the cultural geography of non-redeemed creation. In this sense, the church points to the intersection of the Spirit of God with created culture.

In conclusion, from a *Spirit-friendly* postmodern perspective, the most appropriate category to speak of the church is that of culture. Consequently, *the culture of the Spirit* is to be the *locus theologicus*—the primal location for God's self-disclosure, human self-disclosure, and theological reflection. Correspondingly, it is possible to speak of God in a postmodern context, using postmodern language, insofar as such a language is complemented with a theology of creation. A theology of creation can expand the postmodern language to include the language of the Spirit of God, Christ's Spirit, making a postmodern approach *Spirit-friendly*.

Conclusions

Our analysis has concurred with Latino/a theologizing in that culture is to be regarded a primal category for theological reflection. In other words, *acultural* theological reflection is only a possibility for an uncommitted and *unsituated* mind. Because culture is so essential for the

126. Ibid., 82–83.
127. Ibid., 84–85.
128. Ibid., 82.

process of theological reflection, we proceeded in our analysis with an attitude of cultural suspicion and hope.

We ventured to represent Latino/a theological journey by means of three typological stages, *founders, builders,* and *shapers.* We thought of this kind of metaphorical horizon wishing to show that Latino/a theology is *a home* in constant development, a *journey* of critical faith of the few who have taken seriously the task of learning life and religion from the hands of the many, the Latino/a people.

After surveying influential Latino/a theologians from both traditions, Roman Catholic and Protestant, we concluded that Latino/a theologizing has used the concept of culture with a modern understanding in mind. As such, Latino/a theologizing (as a whole) left the *historical transcendent Spirit* of God outside the realm of primary reflection, many times subduing it to historical-immanent modern categories and practices or relegating it merely as "a Pentecostal perspective." In lieu of this fact, we sought alternative categories for understanding culture having a more open and relevant paradigm, one that could allow us to speak theologically about God in a historical-transcendent fashion and to speak about Latino/a culture in diverse and fluid terms.

We found that the postmodern categories of *embodiment, relationality, and transmissibility* complied with our perception of Latino/a life particularly in urban settings and thus provided an attractive alternative to speaking about the culture-making process, heterogeneity, and fluidity as encountered in urban forms of life of the Latino/a people. Yet, one issue remained as unresolved, namely how to speak about God as the historical-transcendent cultural subject within postmodern language.

Assisted by Alex García-Rivera and William Dyrness, we were able to discern a postmodern *Spirit-friendly* cultural paradigm, one that integrated a postmodern perception of the human experience and a theology of creation. In such a paradigm, we discerned a *"created invisible"* space serving as the basis for the experience and language of the Spirit. The nature of the experience, as postmodern approaches suggest, is intersubjective, where the human subject encounters the *historical transcendent Spirit* as a *subject* and *narrator* or *referral* of God's Big story. In this sense, we suggested, the *"created* invisible*"* refers to the *realm of the experience of the Spirit.* In such a realm there is the possibility of turning toward God, of interpreting God's story as witnessed by Scriptures, of becoming new creation in Jesus Christ, and of imagining transformative cultural practices that are to be *made visible* by the Christian community—the *created* visible culture of the Spirit.

In this way, we have attempted to show how Latino/a theology can continue moving toward a *transformational discourse*—one that may culturally witness to Jesus—by expanding its modern understanding of culture to include the historical transcendent Spirit of Christ. Having identified the culture of the Spirit, as the *primal locus theologicus* for Latino/a theologizing, we are required to show how this cultural perspective informs our ecclesiological vision. This is the task we venture to take on the next chapter.

3

The Pentecost and the Cross as the Authoring Narratives of the Cruciform Community of the Spirit

In our previous chapter, we suggested that Latino/a theologizing must reflect explicitly on the Spirit of Christ as the *historical transcendent* cultural subject that validates culture as *locus theologicus*; this indeed is a valid suggestion for any theological discourse today. We envision, therefore, the *culture* of the Spirit as the intersection and juncture of God's Spirit with *created* visible culture. We are referring, herein, not to an abstract category but to a concrete, historical, and domestic relational realm, the church. The church is, in its cultural essence, embodiment, relationality, and trans-mission. That is, the church is the embodiment of the message of Jesus Christ, made visible in community through the relationality of the Spirit of Christ and the intersubjective relationality of the people of God, with the mission of perpetuating meaningful life—as the practice of Christ's peace—within the cultural geography of non-redeemed creation.

The Spirit of God is the divine *rhetorician,* the perpetual originator of Christian experience and authentic transformation. If Latino/a theology is to account for God's *pneumaloquence*[1] in its theological process and serve as *theologia a Deo docetur, Deum docet, et ad Deum ducit,*[2] then Latino/a theology must culturally imagine the church as a transformational communal parlance—the culture of the Spirit. This is the central vision of our entire work. In accord with this vision, then, we suggest in this chapter that Latino/a theology shall develop a

1. *Pneumaloquence* is a term I created to speak of the Spirit's eloquent intent to persuade the human subject in favor of God's ultimate purpose and destiny.

2. "Theology is taught by God, teaches of God, and leads to God."

critical ecclesiology by focusing on the biblical narratives of the Pentecost and the cross—embodied in community—as the convergent matrix for understanding the church as the culture of the Spirit.

In the following pages, we shall acknowledge the Spirit as the divine *rhetorician* whose *pneumaloquence* has inaugurated the *era of the Spirit*, persuading influential theologians across time and history to become aware of his historical role. The *era of the Spirit* reveals the continuing praxis of the Spirit as *Christopraxis*. Secondly, we shall explore the biblical narrative of the Pentecost as the entry point and shaping force of Christian experience. Such an experience takes place within the realm of the *created* invisible—the intersection of the Spirit and created culture—disclosing a polyphonic language, while affirming cultural diversity. Thirdly, we shall further extend the understanding of the Pentecost to include the communal meaning of the cross (cruciformity). The church, then, is to be perceived as the embodiment of the Pentecost and the cross, functioning as the *cruciform community of the Spirit*. Finally, the Christian community is envisioned as God's cultural agent of transformation—within culture at large—or God's communal transformational parlance.

Pneumaloquence and the Era of the Spirit

> At the beginning of this century a Christian observer stands facing something completely new in the history of Christianity. The numerical balance of forces of the Christian presence in the world has been radically altered. By contrast with the early twenty century, when large churches and missionary strength were growing in Europe and North America, today the practice of Christian faith is declining rapidly in Europe while the churches in Africa and Latin America are growing vigorously. . . . It is acknowledged that missionary drive has shifted to the South. Even though the African and Latin American churches are poor and are facing dramatic challenges as a result of the social and economic crisis in their regions, they are sending missionaries to other parts of the world.[3]

Reading this paragraph suggests a question: How can impoverished communities become sources of *mission* and *agents of transformation*? Given the indubitable poverty and injustice permeating Latin

3. Escobar, *Changing Tides*, 7.

American settings, how are these communities managing to survive and even serve (do missions) graciously amid other, more economically stable settings?

Love seems to be an appealing answer. The language of love, in Gustavo Gutiérrez's perception, is at the heart of liberation theologizing. The historical reality of poverty and injustice, amidst the people of Latin America, moved a community of (liberation) theologians to ask: *how to speak of God as loving father in an inhuman world?* The experience of poverty and sociopolitical injustice, then, pointed to the rhetoric of love as grasped by this theological discourse. The experience of poverty—always a concrete experience—voiced a message in the form of a question. The question became a language. A community of theologians began to articulate that language and then began asking questions—historical, theological, political, ecclesiastical, sociological, and so on. Today we know this language as liberation theology. As Gutiérrez explains, it is based on a question.[4] Detractors and admirers alike admit that this discourse, this question, has marked theology forever. Yet, unfortunately, Latin America continues to be poor and unjust power structures continue to rule. In Latin America, devastated social settings constitute an environment where violence is used as a mechanism of social survival for many segments of society (e.g., gangs, police and military corruption, black market, etc.).

The Spirit of Christ, as well as poverty, also has an historical *form* which can be experienced *as* cultural *variations* and *persuasions.*[5] While

4. See ch. 1 pp. 10–11 above.

5. Our use of the Spirit of Christ, as we have anticipated in our introduction, reflects a dynamic Christology or a pneumatological Christology. On the one hand, we understand that Jesus' specific personhood (individuation) resides in God's glory; his specific personhood is at the right hand of the Father until the *parousia* (Rom 8.34; Acts 7.56; Col 3.1; Heb 10.12; 1 Pet 3.22). On the other hand, theologians such as Barth, Moltmann, and particularly Bonhoeffer have asked how we can know Jesus Christ concretely. In the case of Bonhoeffer, the answer points to "the community of the saints" as the collective person of Christ (*Sanctorum Communio*). Such an understanding appeals to our sociological and anthropological intelligence, in light of our current analysis. Human beings are de facto relational beings. So, can we authentically apprehend Jesus otherwise (e.g., as doctrine [*nous*] or as action [*poiesis/praxis*] or experience [*aistesis*])? If we opt for doctrine as a primary category, we are in line for idealism and rationalism, of which much reformed theology and evangelicalism in general is guilty. If we opt for action as the primary category, we are in line for anthropologism/humanism in many forms (including extreme sacramentalism and human liberationism). If we opt for experience as the primary category, we are in line with liberal-empathetic Protestantism.

the experience of poverty, in itself, is a consequence of evil and unjust power structures, it should also be admitted that poverty constitutes a deploying platform of further injustice, oppression, victimization, absence of love and of peace. Indeed, such an experience of immanent poverty makes one very vulnerable to the temptation of violence. It is very appealing for those experiencing oppression and those advocating for them to respond with acts of violence as a means of survival and liberation. The experience of the Spirit of Christ, alternatively, persuades us by means of inclusiveness, affirmations of our various stories, and hope. The language of the Spirit—love, joy, and futurity—appeals to us in a rather different manner than that of poverty and violence. The rhetoric of the Spirit persuades us not outside our immediate historical condition by promising a socially-constructed utopia. The rhetoric of the Spirit finds an appeal in the midst of poverty, injustice, and violence by means of creating a *new space for survival* and *hope*, by creating a *new experience* where every aspect of life is affected by love, joy, and futurity. In this sense, we can speak of *pneumaloquence* as the aesthetic language of the Spirit of Christ by which it persuades us to experience *love, joy, and futurity* in the *created* invisible.

Ray Anderson's view of praxis as including "telos in action" (acted *nous*) seems a middle point (see Anderson, *The Shape of Practical Theology*, 48–60.). It seems that Anderson's view is consequence of Barth's struggle with Kantian rejection of pure knowledge as human possibility. Barth's solution suggests that God accommodates his being in action (revelation=God's action). Part of the issue is accepting to what extent God's Spirit, the Holy Spirit, and the Spirit of the resurrected Christ are one and the same. The *filioque* clause controversy—where the church of the West unilaterally adopted the phrase "from the Father and the Son" with regard to the Trinitarian economy, has created tensions. However, the relationship of the Holy Spirit and Christ's Spirit has been clarified in favor of the fact that they are one and the same. New Testament scholars such as James Dunn, Gordon Fee, and Michael Gorman, among many others, seem to concur with this understanding. Gorman, especially, depends on this Christological-pneumatological identification (see Gorman, *Cruciformity*, 50–62.). If one accepts this understanding then we could see Jesus as pluriformic (see Greene, *Christology in Cultural Perspective* and Hart, *The Beauty of the Infinite*). In his individuation Jesus Christ is at the right hand of the Father; in his relationality Jesus Christ and "his body" (community of the saints) are apprehended as one; in his eschatological presence Jesus' Spirit appears as the Holy Spirit (Moltmann, Gorman); and perhaps in his quintessential presence Jesus is the unifying force of the cosmos. Even the late John H. Yoder points to this possibility in "Armaments and Eschatology."

Today's missiological perception of Christianity suggests, as Samuel Escobar's words have described,[6] that we are living in exciting times. It is a time when violence has encountered an enemy. Violence in its *variations* (e.g., poverty, injustice, exploitation, exclusion, etc.) loses *historical* territory as the Spirit of Christ moves through human history in and through the church. Some have ventured to describe this historical and cultural trajectory of the Spirit (between Jesus' resurrection and *parousia*) as "the era of the Spirit."[7]

God as *sustainer* has been involved with creation and its perpetual processes since the beginning.[8] God as *renewer*, similarly, moves within the juncture of two histories, the history of the Spirit and the history of humanity. Jürgen Moltmann's perception in this regard is clever:

> Faith in Christ and hope for the kingdom are due to the presence of God in the Spirit. The church understands the tension between faith and hope as the history of the Spirit that makes all things new. Its fellowship with Christ is founded on the experience of the Spirit which manifests Christ, unites us with him and glorifies him in men.[9]

The church is, we have argued, the cultural geography of the Spirit, representing a crossroads where the Big story of God meet the various stories of people in real history.[10] The big story of God is told rhetorically or with a *pneumaloquence* in the context of human history and culture, thus invigorating cultures, nations, cities, barrios, and ghettoes. The praxis of the Spirit in culture, whose *pneumaloquence* can be experienced as love, joy, and futurity, constitutes a hermeneutical horizon, a preferred optic through which we are to see and understand Christian experience and the church. Leonardo Boff, a liberation theologian (of the Spirit), acknowledges this fact: "When we say that we live in the era of the Holy Spirit, we are affirming that the Spirit constitutes the frontal reality out of which we are to interpret our salvific situation."[11] This era of the Spirit is *an historical* and *cultural* era, for the salvific situation,

---

6. See p. 71 n 3 above.

7. See Boff, *Gracia y Experiencia*, 266–67.

8. See Dyrness, *The Earth is God's*, ch. 3.

9. Moltmann, *The Church in the Power of the Spirit*, 197.

10. García-Rivera, Alex. "Creator of the Visible," 55.

11. Boff, *Gracia y Experiencia*, 267.

as Boff puts it, is necessarily an historical and cultural experience. To such an era shall correspond a theological rhetoric that allows for the persuasion of the Spirit. Boff seems to consent to such a persuasion by suggesting that out of this "experiencing of the Spirit" we are to practice and reflect about our faith.

Other influential theologians have also acknowledged the insinuations of the Spirit of God in light of a Spirit-informed theological reflection—although with various agendas in mind. The Eastern Fathers, for instance, fought against pneumatological heresies (e.g., *pneumatochamoi*), gave the Spirit a sacramental rank (e.g., *epiclesis*), spoke of the Holy Spirit in Trinitarian categories (*perichoresis*), and thought of the Spirit in soteriological terms (*theosis*).[12] In the case of the Latin tradition, Augustine was persuaded that the best way to understand and speak of the Spirit was through a kind of aesthetic rather than rational language. Hence, for Augustine *love* is the primal theological category to speak of the presence and action of the Spirit in the human realm.[13] This primordial aesthetic language impacted, positively and negatively, future visions of the Spirit in medieval, modern, and even postmodern theological ventures.[14]

The experience of the Spirit entered the modern era under the rubrics of aesthetic-mystical experiences, thus two ideological projects found their way in to provide for a different route: the transcendentalism of Hegel and Kant, and the liberalism headed by Schleiermacher and his heirs. The former, particularly Hegel, appropriated the concept of the Spirit for the sake of reason at the expense of transcendence. Hegel's spirit (geist) was fully historical, or better said, it was historical reason or *intellectus*. The liberal school, on the other hand, epitomized the modern conception of aesthetics by making the Spirit a category of the human *subject*. In this sense, the Spirit represented an influence, a coherence that allowed for God-consciousness in the human subject, only meaningful when studied in relationship to the church and the

---

12. See Kärkkäinen, *Pneumatology*, 43–46.

13. Ibid., 46–48.

14. In the medieval period, the Spirit fell into the experiential category of the spiritual senses in the influential works of, for instance, Bernard of Clairvaux, Bonaventure, and Catherine of Siena. See ibid., 49–55. For a postmodern use of Augustine's concept of love (which we tend to favor) see, Hart, *The Beauty of the Infinity*.

world, not by itself—for the *historical* dominated the agenda of modern liberal theology.[15]

A critical reaction against the modern liberal agenda toward the Spirit was launched by Karl Barth.[16] A consistent reading of Barth will exhibit his radical view of revelation as a concrete act of God's self-disclosure in human history.[17] God is the subject who objectivizes himself in human history, thus God should be, in Barth's view, the object of study of theological inquiry.[18] In the same way, Barth defends a "pneumatological biblical exegesis,"[19] underlining the "pneumatological character" of Christian theology—a character that, to a significant extent, determines the validity of theology itself. Thus, Barth declares, "The best theology (not to speak of the only right one) of the highest, or even the exclusively true and real, God would have the following distinction: it would *prove* itself—by the demonstration of the Spirit and of its power."[20] Barth, herein, seems to echo St. Paul's experience of the Spirit as recorded, for example, in 1 Cor 2. Barth was claiming, indeed, that if we are in the business of looking (literally, competing) for an authentic and true theology then such a theology must be an expression of God himself as revealed by his Spirit.

From the standpoint of contemporary missiology, the Latin American theologian, Samuel Escobar acknowledges that the spectacular development and growth of Pentecostal/Charismatic movements in Latin American today is due not to a human factor but to the fact that Wesleyan and Moravian missionaries included in the genome of Latin American Protestantism, the chromosome of the Holy Spirit.[21]

Robert Schreiter, when elaborating on contextual/local theology—a theology that is a byproduct of the dynamic and complex interaction of the Gospel, the Church, and Culture—acknowledges that the praxis of the Spirit in a given context is a shaping factor. The shaping force or "movements of the Spirit" affects, in a constructive way, cultural realities

15. Kärkkäinen, *Pneumatology*, 62–65.

16. See the first essay in Barth, *The Humanity of God*.

17. An excellent contemporary discussion on the matter of Barth's understanding of "Truth as self-involving" is developed in George Hunsinger, *Disruptive Grace*, 305–37.

18. Barth, "The Place of Theology," 26.

19. Burnett, *Karl Barth's Theological Exegesis*, ch. 4.

20. Barth, "The Place of Theology," 23.

21. Escobar, *Changing Tides*, 137.

through the gospel of Jesus Christ as articulated by the body of Christ. Schreiter comments,

> Another way of speaking about this context created by the movement of the Spirit and by the power of the gospel in a community is that it creates a certain spirituality among believers. A way to God is charted out, a pathway to deeper faith and commitment opens out before the community. The pathway provides the essential context within which the local theology is then developed. Theology has to be more than an acute analysis of culture and tradition. It is always done for the sake of a community.[22]

Schreiter seems to acknowledge the primacy of the Spirit in theological elaboration, not as a variable but as a formative factor. Thus for Schreiter, "one cannot speak of a community developing a local theology without its being filled with the Spirit and working under the power of the gospel."[23]

From a U.S. Latino/a perspective, the Pentecostal theologian, Eldin Villafañe speaks to the significance of the Spirit on Christian ethics as follows:

> Ethics in Hispanic Pentecostalism emerges from its experience of the Spirit. The love of God in Jesus Christ poured out by the Spirit begins the spiritual pilgrimage (Rom 5:5). This love becomes the source, motive and power of the living in the Spirit. It is this transforming experience of love that challenges the believer to seek "in obedience to God to follow Jesus in the power of the Spirit." This is both a spirituality and an ethic of the Spirit.[24]

Villafañe understands here that it is from the experience of love by the Spirit that one acquires "theological understanding" and "ethical social praxis." That is, the Spirit "pours" love into our hearts, consequently, we initiate our "pilgrimage" in obedience to follow Jesus. Following Jesus is never possible on our own initiative; it is always based on a *created-situation*. The Spirit is who calls us and by so doing a *new situation* is created—to which we must respond in obedience. In this sense, Bonhoeffer's observation is appropriate: "Unless [we] obey [we] cannot

22. Schreiter. *Constructing Local Theologies*, 24.

23. Ibid.

24. Villafañe, *The Liberating Spirit*, 194–95.

believe."[25] Faith is not what creates the situation, explains Bonhoeffer, but the other way around. The experience of the Spirit reveals, in our opinion, the divine rhetoric of love, joy, and futurity.

In conclusion, *insinuations* of the Spirit as *love*, for instance, are grasped with some easiness in pre-modern times, yet, with some hesitation in modernity due to the *historical* agenda mediating the theological process. Secondly, we can say that the theologians discussed in this section attest—in their various contexts, traditions, and agendas—to the significance of the praxis of the Spirit in history and culture. The experience of the Spirit, as Boff notices, is Christ's "graced experience."[26]

The *era of the Spirit* shall continue until the *parousia*. Meanwhile, the Spirit continues to persuade the human *form* (culture) with insinuations of love, joy, and futurity expressed, ecclesiologically, in *variations* of inclusiveness, community, and hope. A theology that corresponds to this *pneumaloquence* is, we claim, *a theology of the Spirit*. Such a theology acknowledges the rhetoric and praxis of the Spirit of Christ in history and culture. We will next explore the Pentecost event as described in the New Testament and its ecclesiological implications for *a theology of the Spirit*.

Pentecost and the Shaping of Christian Experience

> When the day of Pentecost had come, they were all together in one place. And suddenly from heaven there came a sound like the rush of a violent wind, and it filled the entire house where they were sitting. Divided tongues, as of fire, appeared among them, and a tongue rested on each of them. *All of them were filled with the Holy Spirit and began to speak in other languages, as the Spirit gave them ability.* Now there were devout Jews from every nation under heaven living in Jerusalem. And at this sound the crowd gathered and was bewildered, because each one heard them speaking in the native language of each. Amazed and astonished, they asked, "Are not all these who are speaking Galileans? And how is it that we hear, each of us, in our own native language? Parthians, Medes, Elamites, and residents of Mesopotamia, Judea and Cappadocia, Pontus and Asia, Phrygia and Pamphylia, Egypt and the parts of Libya belonging to Cyrene, and visitors from Rome, both Jews and proselytes,

25. Bonhoeffer, *The Cost of Discipleship*, 72.

26. Boff, *Gracia y Experiencia*, 262–74.

Cretans and Arabs—in our own languages *we hear them speaking about God's deeds of power.*" (Acts 2:1-11, emphasis added)

Pentecost is a biblical narrative—Big story—that tells about the human experience in the *created* invisible realm, the juncture where Christ's Spirit intersects human culture. Pentecost conveys a rhetoric that points beyond human language and understanding. It points to a divine rhetoric, the language of *God's deeds of power* (τὰ μεγαλεῖα τους θεου). We have previously referred to this rhetoric as *pneumaloquence*. This rhetoric accepts no imitation on anthropological grounds. The language of the Spirit, which speaks the mighty works of God, is *unnatural* to the human subject and divergent in content, form, and intention to any human *extravagant speech.* However, translation and transmission is available, so argues the apostle Paul:

> My speech and my proclamation were not with plausible words of wisdom ("eloquence" in NIV), but with a demonstration of the Spirit and of power, so that your faith might rest not on human wisdom but on the power of God . . .
> We speak God's wisdom, secret and hidden, which God decreed before the ages for our glory. None of the rulers of this age understood this; for if they had, they would not have crucified the Lord of glory. But, as it is written, "What no eye has seen, nor ear heard, nor the human heart conceived, what God has prepared for those who love him"—these things God has revealed to us through the Spirit; for the Spirit searches everything, even the depths of God. (1 Cor 2:4, 5, 7-10)

The translation and transmission of such a language to the human subject is, as Paul explains, the particular task of the Spirit. This *unnatural* phenomenon is at the core of the Pentecost experience. The Spirit discloses a polyphonic and polyglot personality that makes God's deeds of power meaningful to the hearers—as a polyphonic experience of intersubjective nature. This type of experience, as we have suggested, is best understood within the coordinates of a *Spirit-friendly postmodern plane,* for it originates within the realm of the *created* invisible and operates within a *triadic* sign system. In this sense, the intersubjective *différance,* which is confusing and non-intelligible, requires a *renvoi* or referral—the Spirit. Linguistic clarity and intelligibility, within these experiential coordinates, are impossible on anthropological grounds, thus requiring translation or narration. The Holy Spirit, then, is the narrator and interpreter of God's Big story in interrelation with us and our stories.

Under these conditions, we might find an advantage for making sense of Paul's claim that revelation (ἀπεκάλυψεν—"made visible, available, translate")[27] comes *through* the Spirit, as the Spirit interrelates (ἐραυνα—"penetrates, examine")[28] the depths (βάθη—"essence, being, Self-story")[29] of God with our own spirit (self-story). This type of claim finds meaning within our *Spirit-friendly* postmodern approach. Spirit-to-(human) spirit experience—intersubjective relationality—is further illustrated in Paul's following words:

> Now we have received not the spirit of the world, but the Spirit that is from God, so that we may understand the gifts bestowed on us by God. And we speak of these things in words not taught by human wisdom but taught by the Spirit, interpreting spiritual things to those who are spiritual. (1 Cor 2:12–13)

The intersubjective relationality of the Spirit of Christ with the human spirit in the realm of the *created* invisible—an experiential realm—is God's way of persuading the human subject with a rhetoric of love, joy, and hope. In love (*agape*), we find acceptance, inclusion, and affirmation of our various and sometimes confusing stories. In joy (*chara*), we find an opportunity for social engagement—in community—because of Jesus Christ's resurrection, hence, the most ancient greeting among Christians was: Jesus has risen! Certainly, he has risen! In hope (*elpis*), we find *mañana* (future), possibility, and empowerment. We believe these parameters conform the matrix by which we shall understand the Pentecost as a formative biblical story—Big story—of the Spirit of Christ intersecting human culture. As result, the Christian community comes to existence and is made visible.

Pentecost is about Inclusion and Affirmation in Christ

The *historical* Pentecost, happened in a very human and cultural way—for humanity necessarily *happens* in a cultural way.[30] Pentecost presents us with a vision in which God affirms cultural existence in its variety

27 Rienecker and Rogers, *Linguistic Key*, 391.

28. Ibid.

29. Ibid., 392.

30. Espín, "Grace and Humanness," 138–55; Anderson, *On Being Human*, 167.

and fluidity. It was *pentecostes* (Heb. Shavu'ot), a major cultural festivity for the Jewish community: "the festival of firstfruits of the wheat-harvest";[31] the celebration of the "giving of Our Torah" (Exod 23, Lev 23, Num 28, Deut 16).[32] Pentecost was a day when the "season of the giving of Our Torah" was given a new communal content and eschatological interpretation; it became the "season of the giving of the Spirit."

From a biblical perspective, the Pentecost story points to *cultural creation*. The author of the book of Acts, we maintain, points to this fact. Ralph Martin assesses many of the speculations held by New Testament experts who try to figure out what might have been Luke's purpose behind the book of Acts. Some see a "historical" motivation evidenced by laborious data, *ancient* first-rate chronological accounts,[33] and sharp biographical literary constructions.[34] Others prefer the theological (kerygmatic) route arguing that Luke was using historical mechanisms "as a vehicle to edify the church of his day."[35] Martin, himself, shows preference for a rather "pastoral" motivation in Luke's literary production: "Luke's interests are not speculative or even theological; rather, they are pastorally motivated."[36] Given Luke's proximity to Paul's theological views and pastoral practice, as portrayed by the book of Acts and Pauline literature,[37] one cannot help but think of a more *relevant* purpose for the book of Acts: *a pastoral-theological document*. This perception interrelates the historical, kerygmatic, and pastoral motivations in a way that dialectically integrates practical issues addressed kerygmatically in a particular context. Raymond Brown, the distinguished Catholic New Testament scholar, seems to underscore this *pastoral-theological* perception: "In Acts the narrative he [Luke] recounts is primarily intended to give believers assurance (Luke 1:4) and strengthen

---

31. Bruce, *The Acts of the Apostles*, 81.

32. See "Shavu'ot."

33. For support on this single point see Brown, *An Introduction to the New Testament*, 321–22.

34. Here, New Testament experts such as Bruce, Meyer, and Ramsay follow this view. See Martin, *New Testament Foundations*, 53–58.

35. Ibid, 54.

36. Ibid, 57.

37. See for instance the affective manner Paul speaks of Luke (Col 4:14; 2 Tim 4:11) and the way Luke himself is involved in the narrative in the so-called "we passages" of Acts (11:28; 16:10–17; 20:5–21; 21:18; 27:1—28:6).

with theological insight. Therefore, whatever history Acts preserves is put to the service of theology and pastoral preaching."[38] In addition, when discerning the dominant themes of the Acts, one of these themes supports our perception, namely, "the church, as a socio-religious community, came out of Judaism."[39] Hence, the Christian community was born historically, theologically, and culturally at the Pentecost Story. Although emerging "out of" an existing culture (Jewish), it becomes a new cultural community.

Now, the church though Jewish by origin and context, transforms at Pentecost into a polyphonic-multiracial cultural community.[40] The Pentecost is the *formative biblical narrative* revealing how the Spirit intersected a cultural milieu, respecting, embracing, and affirming its various and multiple stories and identities. Such a diverse socio-cultural setting is portrayed with the following words: "and began to speak in other tongues . . . there were dwelling in Jerusalem Jews, devout men from every nation under heaven . . . they were bewildered, because each one heard them speak in his own language" (Acts 2:4–6 [RSV]). The Pentecost Story offers, then, a rich cultural vision in which a diverse cultural geography was constructed by the power of the Spirit into the Christian community.

The Pentecost Story describes a new creation, thus, a new beginning, which leads to cultural *affirmation* and *inclusion*. The idea that New Testament Judaism was a homogeneous cultural community, a monolithic culture, is erroneous. J. D. G. Dunn, in his work *Christianity in the Making*, has convincingly shown how Jewish pseudepigrapha and the writings of Philo present an alternative reading of the *diversity* of the Jewish people, in contrast to the accepted perception of "normative Judaism" or the rabbinic portrayal of "Mishnahic/Talmudic Judaism."[41] Dunn states the case where Jesus of Nazareth and the emerging church are situated within the Second Temple period, a time when Jewish self-perception was struggling with identity issues at the edge of a diverse cultural matrix.[42] Cultural diversity, and consequently self-perception

38. Brown, *An Introduction to the New Testament*, 322.

39. Martin, *New Testament Foundations*, 61.

40. Ibid. See also Acts 1:8; 2:1–13; 10; and 13, where we see the cultural construction of the multiracial, multiethnic church.

41. See Dunn, *Christianity in the Making*, 255–86.

42. Ibid, 260.

issues, were part of the cultural milieu within which the Christian community—the church—emerged. Then, naturally, the praxis of the Spirit is portrayed in the book of Acts—indeed, the rest of the New Testament—as a praxis of affirmation, unity, and mission or *inclusion, community, and transmission.* Here, Raymond Brown's understanding of Acts is substantial by suggesting that the Pentecost Story discloses the "renewal of God's covenant and the affirmation of the [Jewish and non-Jewish] church as God's own people."[43] Even more significant is Brown's observation that the *Old Testament Pentecost* (Exodus 19) shows that YHWH affirmed the Jews, but not the non-Jewish people as God's own (by the covenant and the Law). However, the *Pentecost Story* of Acts 2, as presented after the missiological statement of Acts 1:8, presents a vision of *inclusion, community, and transmission* as it points to the affirmation of *all people's* languages and cultures (stories)—Jews and non-Jews—who are willing to receive the Spirit of God. Peter's quote of Joel 2:28–32 (Acts 2:17–21) and the historical happenings narrated by the rest of Acts signal this fact. Thus, it makes sense to argue that the basis of unity in the body of Christ resides in the Spirit and its praxis of commonality and transmission. In this regard, the practical theologian Ray Anderson rightly commends, "The church is constantly being re-created through the mission of the Spirit. At the same time it has historical and ecclesial continuity and universality through the Spirit."[44] Anderson refers here to his understanding of Christopraxis, that is, the Pentecost-based process of church-making in history by the praxis of the Spirit.[45] Said differently, the Church of Jesus Christ emerges as the Spirit re-tells people's stories in intersection with Christ's grand narrative, unifying diversity, and perpetuating the meaningful Big story of Christ over time.

A quick review of precarious missiological situations in the book of Acts can help us see the significance of Anderson's view. When the cultural values of a group (for instance the new converts of Asia Minor) was threatened by apodictic forms of Christian Judaism, the Spirit acted

43. Brown, *An Introduction to the New Testament.* 284.

44. See Anderson, *Ministry on the Fireline,* 126.

45. Colin J. Greene makes use of *christopraxis* in a similar way to Anderson. He views *christopraxis* as a way to know the Messiah as we are committed to, and immersed on, his Messianic mission to the world (Greene, *Christology in Cultural Perspective,* 21, 22, 349).

upon the main church leaders in order to resist any kind of "cultural destruction." A typical case is found in Acts 15. The Christian faith had been expanding to the Gentile world ("the end of the earth . . ."). One of the Jewish Christian groups had understood the Law of Moses as a precondition for Christian conversion. So, the Jerusalem Christian conference met to seek a resolution to the matter. The Jerusalem Christian leaders accepted the praxis of the Spirit—a praxis manifested by visions (see Peter in Acts 10), wonders and signs among Gentiles (see Peter, Paul, Barnabas in Acts 13–14), and Scriptural interpretation (see the conference as the body of Christ in Acts 15)—as the proper praxis to resolving this matter. They concluded, "it has seemed good to the Holy Spirit and to us to lay upon you no greater burden" (Acts 15:28).

In the pre-Easter ministry of the disciples, it was Jesus himself who mediated such matters (see for instance, Luke 9:10–17, 51–55; Matt 17:14–22). After Easter, it was still the praxis of Jesus Christ (Christopraxis)—yet in the presence of the Spirit—who continued holding together the Christian community. In Anderson's words, "We cannot have Pentecost without Christ . . . Pentecost is Christ's parousia, his manifestation in the world, empowering his disciples with his presence as they bear witness to him to the ends of the earth."[46] Following Anderson's logic, the Pentecost Story as the inauguration and continuity of the *era of the Spirit* (until the fullness of the *parousia*), therefore, shall be understood as the *entry point and the shaping force of Christian experience*. This implies that the Pentecost Story is God's chosen Story for authoring Christian experience and is, thus, formative for Christian faith. Also, Pentecost points to God's chosen praxis, that is, Christopraxis: the practice of *inclusion* in love, the practice of *community* in joy, and the practice of *transmission* or futurity in hope.

Christopraxis, as we have presented it, gathers multiple intelligences and practices in the form of natural reasoning, common sense, and communal interpretation of Scripture, and supra-natural perceptions and works (visions, signs, wonders, charisms, etc.) as mediated by aesthetic judgment (αἰσθητήριον, Heb 5:14).[47] Furthermore, the

---

46. Anderson, *Ministry on the Fireline*, 38.

47. Delling, "αἰσθάνομαι, αἴσθησις, αἰσθητήριον," *Theological Dictionary of the New Testament* 1:187–88. A parallel understanding of Christopraxis, as we see it, could also be discerned in the thought of Father De Caussade, a Jesuit spiritual director, who already in the early 1700s was developing a Christological vision where the

Pentecost Story continues to validate and shape Christian character until the fullness of the *parousia*. Pentecost Story, for this matter, is not about a particular historical church trapped in a historical monad, which, passing such a monad, ceased to experience the *pneumaloquence* of the Spirit. Pentecost is about Christ's presence in the Spirit in the midst of cultural realities, affirming, shaping, and empowering the human subject in community and individuation (reason, emotiveness, sociability, spirituality, behavior, etc.). Consequently, we cannot call *an experience* a Christian experience if such an *experience is not authored* by the Spirit of God.[48]

Further ecclesiological consequences derive from this theological understanding, namely, ministry, mission, social transformation, ethics, and similar Christian items must be shaped by the Spirit in a *Pentecost way*. Again, Anderson articulates it eloquently: "I view Pentecost as the pivotal point of faith from which we can look back to the incarnation of God in Jesus of Nazareth and look forward into our contemporary life and witness to Jesus Christ in the world."[49] We must only re-emphasize that God, in his Spirit, acts at the core of cultural life; the concept of the world is not *acultural*.

In sum, the *emerging church* of the first century discloses how a diverse and heterogeneous community was affirmed and culturally stretched to include non-Jews ("the ends of the earth" Acts 1:8), as the people experienced the Spirit's unifying force and were persuaded by the *pneumaloquence* of the Spirit of the resurrected Christ. The Pentecost Story continues to be formative for Christian experience and meets us at the privileged realm of the *created* invisible, where our stories are intersected by the Spirit, where the polyphonic experience of the Spirit affirms our identities and gives us a *mañana* (future) in God. In the *created* invisible, the real of the Spirit, there is the possibility of turning toward God, of interpreting God's story as witnessed by Scriptures, of becoming a new creation in Jesus Christ, and of imagining

---

"establishment and growth of Jesus Christ in the person's heart" was based on God's mysterious grace and the person's domestic praxis of obedience to her/his duties in the present moment as determined by God (see de Caussade, *The Sacrament of the Present Moment*, 43–44). Such an understanding can be extended to represent church praxis, in which case it would pair with our view more precisely.

48. See Dunn, *The Theology of Paul the Apostle*, 426–34.

49. Anderson, *Ministry on the Fireline*, 23.

.ransformative cultural practices that are to be *made visible* by the Christian community. This is what Michael Gorman refers to when he develops the concept of *cruciformity*. We shall turn next to this understanding.

Cruciformity: The Popular Practice of Pentecost Faith

> For through the law I died to the law, so that I might live to God. I have been crucified with Christ; and it is no longer I who live, but it is Christ who lives in me. And the life I now live in the flesh I live by faith in the Son of God, who loved me and gave himself for me. (Gal 2:20)

Cruciformity—life as conformity to the crucified Jesus—is the visible side of the Pentecost experience. It is the consequence of it. We have suggested that the Pentecost Story is a formative narrative that shapes Christian experience in the *created* invisible space. Cruciformity, as Michael Gorman suggests, is life in community that conforms to the crucified Jesus Christ.[50] Cruciform life is life as embodiment of Jesus' cross in community.[51] Hence, this existential-cultural way of life belongs to the *created visible* realm.

The cross is essentially a secular item. The cross was a vivid and violent reminder of the power of Caesar and the empire, a *visible* symbol of assuring and perpetuating *pax romana*. No one could possibly expect anything good out of the cross—a stumbling block for Jews and foolishness for Gentiles (1 Cor 1:23).[52] Not even in Jesus of Nazareth's case was the cross a positive device for followers and observers. Indeed, it was a sacrament of agony and failure; a demoralizing icon powerful enough to revert the faith of the very apostolic community who represented the new covenant people of God.[53]

50. Michael Gorman is professor of New Testament and early church history at St. Mary's Seminary and University. He is the main promoter of the understanding of "cruciformity." See Gorman, *Cruciformity*.

51. See Ibid., 386.

52. Gorman, from whom we draw the understanding of cruciformity, points to the fact that the crucifixion "was the most miserable of deaths, an accursed thing, a plage." See Ibid., 5.

53. The disciples of Jesus of Nazareth represented, in an embryonic way, the context of the emerging church, later born at Acts 2. We can find support for this reasoning in Hunt, *The Unity of the New Testament*, and Mason, "The New Testament Basis of the Doctrine of the Church."

The cross is, at the same time, "the signature of the one who is risen" (Käsemann).[54] Jesus of Nazareth, in the power of the Spirit, by his praxis of love and obedience to the Father on behalf of humanity gave the cross a divine rhetorical status. The cross had a conversion and reversal in meaning. Jesus Christ did not deprive the cross of its original and secular nuance; it remains as a mark of suffering. This aspect of the cross resembles our humanity, our necessity, our own hopelessness. Jesus Christ added to the cross, however, a redemptive, humanizing, and renewing power. In this sense, we dare to suggest that *the cross was the first to confess/display Jesus as Lord and Savior.* It converted violent punishment into non-violent *peace*—the ultimate and once-for-all act of sacrificial violence.[55] It converted guilt into *forgiveness.* It converted exclusion into *inclusion,* hatred into *love,* deception into *hope.*

The cross' spatial character was also transformed: the place of the "one" became the *form* of the "many"—cruciformity. The cross is, as Simon Weil exclaimed, "infinitely more than martyrdom."[56] Such is the rhetoric of the cross: it is like us to reject it; it is like Jesus Christ to embrace it. The cross is, following Weil's logic, infinitely strange, yet at the same time infinitely familiar. At the juncture of these two trajectories, we find ourselves persuaded by Jesus' cross, by Jesus' way of life.

The apostle Paul swayed by the cross of Jesus dares to replace the sacred Jewish icon of circumcision (a mark of the covenant) for Jesus' cross declaring: "From now on, let no one make trouble for me; for I carry the marks (στίγματα) of Jesus branded on my body" (Gal 6:17).[57] In this context, Paul reacts to those who see the Law as mediation between Gentile believers and Jesus Christ. Though circumcision points to the Law, for Paul the cross is *how* we embrace Jesus' reality. The cross, for Paul, seems to represent a relational space in the concrete. In the re-

---

54. Käsemann, "The Saving Significance," 56; quoted in Gorman, *Cruciformity,* 19.

55. See Girard, *Violence and the Sacred.*

56. Simon Weil, *Gravity and Grace,* 80.

57. There seems to be a consensus among Pauline scholars that Paul based his understanding of Christ on the cross (death and resurrection) and, gravitating around it, he develops his theological positions. See Dunn, *The Theology of Paul the Apostle,* 208–23. See also the allusions to Paul's *theologia crucis* in Bruce, *Paul: Apostle of the Heart Set Free,* 246–47. Significant to our understanding of the cross is the work of Richard B. Hays who views the cross as a dominant (focal) image in Paul's thought—and the New Testament in general. See Hays, *The Moral Vision of the New Testament,* 27–32, 197–205.

lational living of the cross, the believer, Gorman suggests, can conform to cruciform love, cruciform faith, cruciform power, and cruciform hope—in a communal way.[58] Hence, Gorman claims, "fundamentally, cruciformity means community, and community cruciformity."[59] In order to illustrate cruciformity as community and community as cruciformity, we shall turn next to John H. Yoder and his understanding of living according to the cross.

John H. Yoder and the Community of the Cross

Few modern theologians have articulated so well the importance of the cross in the formation of the Christian community as has John Howard Yoder. In the following discussion, we will introduce Yoder's vision of the church in light of the cross, hoping to illustrate how *cruciformity* is the ethical side of the Pentecost Story—the embodiment of the Grand narrative of Jesus lived by the power of the Spirit.

Several have set themselves the task of depicting the central thought of Yoder. Some understand that the theological program of Yoder centered on the fact that "the moral character of God is revealed in Jesus; in his vulnerable love toward the enemy and his resistance to violence."[60] Others see that the seminal thought of the theologian rests on the conception that *Christian ethics is necessarily the ethics of Jesus of Nazareth lived by the Christian community in the world*.[61] Even others, while not denying the previous perspectives, undertake a more scriptural route in approximating the theological reflection of Yoder. They contend that the biblical Jesus is precisely the source of Yoder's theology and ethical perspectives. We take this latter position in our work assuming, with Hays, that for Yoder "the New Testament's portrayal of Jesus must remain the fundamental norm for all Christian ethics."[62]

---

58. Gorman, *Cruciformity* is devoted to this theme. See particularly ch. 5.

59. Ibid., 366.

60. This is argued by Nancey Murphy in Murphy and Ellis, *On the Moral Nature of the Universe*, 178–201. See also Murphy, John Howard Yoder's Systematic Defence," 48–51.

61. Nation, "John H. Yoder," 20–22.

62. Hays, *The Moral Vision of the New Testament*, 252.

Yoder should be read against the context of the dominant ethics of his generation, that of Niebuhr and followers.[63] Yoder understood that much of the content of this mainstream ethics had more to do with *natural theology* than with the *message* of the gospel. Thus, Yoder offers an alternative and "fresh reading of the 'gospel narrative', constantly posing the heuristic question, is there here a social ethic?"[64]

Based on a fine work of New Testament scholarship and endowed with theological creativity, Yoder constructs three major arguments in his *magnus opus* work *The Politics of Jesus*. Hays dissects these arguments as follows:

> (1) The New Testament consistently bears witness to Jesus' renunciation of violence and coercive power; (2) the example of Jesus is directly relevant and normatively binding for the Christian community; (3) faithfulness to the example of Jesus is a political choice, not a withdrawal from the realm of politics.[65]

The Politics of Jesus is then a subversive ethical position against the kind of ethics that proclaimed indifference to Jesus' normative relevance as the source of ethical choice and praxis. Yoder's approach geared him to seek in the gospels narrative, particularly the gospel of Luke, the "political figure of Jesus of Nazareth." He found a Jesus that represented for him an *alternative gestalt* to the existing paradigms of ethical thought and praxis in the political, social, and religious realms.

Jesus' radical discipleship, for Yoder, is pivotal in the creation of an alternative socio-political life. Jesus builds up gradually among his disciples a social reality and a new political order characterized, not by domination and coercive power, but by serving and sharing as the socio-political basis for leadership.[66] In the words of Yoder, "Jesus is . . . calling into being a community of *voluntary* commitment, willing for the sake of its calling to take up upon itself the hostility of the given society . . . [T]o be a disciple is to *share* [emphasis mine] in that style of life of which the cross is the culmination."[67] Yoder, with this insinuation, orients us to the reality of the cross and its ethical implications.

63. I sketch such a context in García-Johnson, "Acentos Eticos de John H. Yoder."

64. Hays, *The Moral Vision of the New Testament*, 240.

65. Ibid., 239–40.

66. Ibid.

67. Quoted in Hays, *The Moral Vision of the New Testament*, 241.

The reality of the cross, for Yoder, is to be present in this earth—here and now—as Jesus' community.[68] Hays sees the cross as Yoder's focal image or dominant hermeneutical metaphor for understanding Jesus earthly life and sociopolitical impact. In other words, the cross is that key metaphor through which every canonical narrative should be read.[69] For Yoder, however, the reality of the cross represents much more than an act of interpretation; it enables us to perform the praxis of social ethics in a prophetic fashion: "Only at one point, only on one subject—but then consistently, universally—is Jesus our example: in his cross."[70]

The cross reflects a normative reality for Yoder. Surely, the cross has a particular dimension with regard to Jesus' atonement. For Yoder, however, the cross demands a "cruciform-shape"[71]—ethical praxis that defines, to a greater extent, the authenticity and faithfulness of the Christian community. This ethical praxis has sociopolitical implications for the Christian community. Indeed, for Yoder an ethic based on the cross gives content and shape to any Christian praxis in society in a way that "the believer's cross must be, like his Lord's, the price of social nonconformity . . . it is the social reality of representing in an unwilling world the Order to Come."[72]

The cross as a norm of ethical praxis suggests an *alternative revolution* that challenges any methodology that centers on violence or coercive power in order to achieve social change. Jesus of Nazareth, insisted Yoder, forthrightly rejected any revolutionary insinuation that utilized violence and coercive power as instruments of social transformation:

> The one temptation the man Jesus faced—and faced again and again—as a constitutive element of his public ministry, was the temptation to exercise social responsibility, in the interest of justified revolution, through the use of available violent methods.[73]

---

68. See Yoder, *The Politics of Jesus*, 51–53.

69. Hays, *The Moral Vision of the New Testament*, 240.

70. Yoder, *The Politics of Jesus*, 95.

71. Gorman interacts with Yoder's understanding of life according to the cross, so cruciformity, in a sense, is a contribution of Yoder's thought to Gorman's work. See Gorman *Cruciformity*, 381.

72. Quoted in Hays, *The Moral Vision of the New Testament*, 243, emphasis original.

73. Yoder, *The Politics of Jesus*, 96.

The alternative of a revolutionary non-violent praxis based on *serving to and sharing with the other*, according to Yoder, is Jesus' political alternative as witnessed by New Testament narrative. The fact that Jesus relinquished any seduction offered by mechanisms of violence attempting to achieve social transformation in his context; the decision not to fight violence with violence revealed the triumph of Jesus over the institutionalized evil of his time. With this non-violent approach Jesus was able to unmask the 'illusion of power' originated by evil and incarnated in political, social, cultural, and religious structures.[74] Nevertheless, complains Yoder, the dominant ethical discourse (of his time and perhaps ours too!) insists in discarding Jesus' praxis as normative for political ethics, pressing themselves to get "our ethics elsewhere, from a responsible calculation of our chances."[75]

In sum, Yoder's vision of the community of the cross is of an incarnational and revolutionary nature, though a non-violent yet subversive cruciform political spirituality is at stake.

The Cruciform Community of the Spirit: a Popular Spirituality

Michael Gorman, who has developed more fully the concept of cruciformity, affirms that cruciformity presupposes the experience of the Spirit:

> The distinctive feature of Paul's experience of the Spirit, and his resulting understanding of the essence of this Spirit, is the paradoxical symbiosis (union) of power and weakness, of power and cruciformity. The charismatic Spirit is also the cruciform Spirit.[76]

From the standpoint of Christian experience, the Pentecost Story precedes cruciformity, for such an experience belongs to the *created* invisible as authored by the Spirit of Christ. Gorman concurs with us in this understanding, underlining that "[t]he Spirit *forms* the Christ-centered

---

74. A discussion entitled "Structured Incredulity" by Yoder gives us an insight into Yoder's position on this matter. See Yoder, Solano, Padilla, and Fraternidad Teológica Latinoamericana, *Iglesia, Etica y Poder*, 14–16.

75. Yoder, *The Politics of Jesus*, 97.

76. Gorman, *Cruciformity*, 52.

community and is *found* in that community."[77] The narrative of the cross, at the same time, is part of that experience yet to be materialized in historical and communal ways. On the horizon of cultural Christian living, cruciformity is the manifestation and embodiment of this experience, for it takes place in the *created visible* realm. With Gorman we reaffirm: *the Spirit of the Pentecost is also the cruciform Spirit*. In this sense, the community of the Spirit is the community of the cross, thus the description "the cruciform community of the Spirit" is appropriate.

The Pentecost Story provides a polyphonic experience to imagine—by *dynamis* and *charismata*—life in an inclusive, loving, joyful, and hoping community. Hence, the Pentecost Story gives the power to live cruciformly (holy, transcending the imperial powers, victorious, and taking the side of the poor and weak).[78] Symbiotically, then, cruciformity is conforming to such an experience, living *lo cotidiano* (daily life) in dynamic correspondence with the Pentecost Story. Cruciformity is living life subversively in culture, in the domestic, having a devotion that is *popular* because it is *created* not just by "the people," but by *God's cruciform people*.

The Christian Community as Culture of the Spirit

The earliest confession of Christian faith—κυριος 'Ιησους—meant nothing less radical than Christ peace, having suffered upon the cross the decisive rejection of the powers of this world, had been raised up by God as the true form of human existence: an eschatologically perfect love, now made invulnerable to all the violences of time, and yet also made incomprehensibly present in the midst of history, because God's final judgment had already befallen the world in the paschal vindication of Jesus of Nazareth. It is only as the offer of this peace within time, as a *real and available practice* that the Christian evangel . . . has any meaning at all; only if the *form* of Christ can be lived out in the community of the church is the confession of the church true; only if Christ can be practiced is Jesus Lord. . . . [I]t is *this presence within time of an eschatological and divine peace,* really incarnate in the person of Jesus and forever *imparted to the body*

77. Ibid., 61.
78. Ibid., 298–303.

of Christ by the power of the Holy Spirit, that remains the very
essence of the church's evangelical *appeal to the world at large.*[79]

Where is authentic transformation in our midst? How are we to
recognize it when we see it? What are the consequences of embracing
it? The Eastern Orthodox theologian David Hart suggests that transformation is a "practice" located within time and history. Should that be
the case, we must then call it a *cultural practice.* This practice, however,
is not a *universal form*; it does not convey a mono-formic model. It is
a practice that reflects a practice that in turn reflects a practice and so
on. In that sense, it is *presence* within time. This presence, though in
history, is not originated of history, that is, it is not an *historical form*
that concretely and specifically portrays the face of transformation for
all settings, cultures, epochs. Instead, it is a presence of eschatological
and divine peace, within time, within culture, within the practice of a
confessing community that makes this presence historical. Thus, the
language and rhetoric of transformation is *divine* peace yet its practice
is *cultural,* as embodied and transmitted by the "Christ-is-Lord" confessing community. Such a practice, insinuates Hart, is the essence of
the evangelical appeal to culture by and large.

The consequence of embracing the *divine* presence of peace in
the logic of Yoder is to live in a way that exhibits *the politics of Jesus.*
The Christian community shall continue Jesus' task of unmasking and
disarming the powers of evil that violently challenge the Lordship of
Jesus Christ.[80]

Yoder's dominant passion, with regard to the church, is his vision
of the church as the moral agent of the kingdom of God in the earth.
Yoder suggests that the church has the mission of modeling and incarnating Jesus' political reality in the world—*as culture.* While much
of mainstream Christian ethics conceives of the church as "a cultural
product different than the kingdom,"[81] Yoder visualizes the church as
"the moral conscience and servant of human society."[82] In its sociocultural role, the church is not merely a shadow or a mere image of the

79. Hart, *The Beauty of the Infinity,* 1–2, emphasis added.

80. Hays, *The Moral Vision of the New Testament,* 244.

81. An excellent compendium of ethical positions is presented in Stassen, Yeager,
Yoder, and Niebuhr, *Authentic Transformation.* See particularly p. 103.

82. Yoder, *The Politics of Jesus,* 155.

spiritual kingdom here on earth. The church, for Yoder, is the "alternative community" the "culture of Christ" that co-exists in prophetic relation to the non-Christian dimension of culture, namely, the secular society.[83] Authentic transformation is achieved, according to Yoder, *in* and *by way of* the Christian community. Thus, the church—as a new social order— is called to find the "[i]nterworld transformational grammar to help us to discern what will need to happen if the collision of the message of Jesus with our pluralistic/relativistic world is to lead to a reconception of the shape of the world."[84]

Cultural transformation or renewal, for Yoder, is part of a process of "reconceptualization" of the cultural codes in a given community or culture. If the church is to function as the sociocultural location for this renewal then a radical commitment to witness to Jesus Christ through the praxis of *serving and sharing* with the greater community/culture is vital. Yoder proposes that "the obedient Christian community [must] become at the same time an instrument for serving and saving the larger culture."[85] Nancey Murphy provides further illumination with regard to the church as a cultural location for renewal:

> The church is a laboratory where we imagine and practice new forms of social life. . . . The church has developed unrivaled social practices that help us maintain and improve the moral character of the community. . . . The church, as an ethical laboratory, can teach the world better ways.[86]

David Hart concurs with Murphy and further argues that the essential language of faith, the *confession* of "Jesus Lord," translates into the essential *practice* of faith, "Christ's peace." The practice of Christ's peace, at the same time, becomes the persuasion, the rhetoric of transformation of the culture at large. Hart is clear in that "only if the *form* of Christ can be lived out in the community of the church is the confession of the church true."[87] Thus, the Christian community—the Jesus Lord (con-

---

83. An impressive interpretation of Yoder in this regard is provided by Duane K. Friesen, *Artists, Citizens, Philosophers,* 52–63.

84. Yoder, *The Priestly Kingdom,* 56.

85. Ibid., 11

86. Murphy, "John Howard Yoder's Systematic Defence of Christian Pacifism," 60–61.

87. Hart, *The Beauty of the Infinite,* 1.

fessing) and Christ's peace (practicing) community—takes the shape of *a transformational communal parlance* in the culture at large.

Conclusions

We have attempted to provide the basis for a critical ecclesiology informed by the biblical narratives of Pentecost and the cross, by a Spirit-friendly postmodern view of culture, and by a dynamic pneumatological Christology that sees the praxis of the Spirit of Christ intersecting culture to produce the polyphonic and diverse culture of the Spirit.

In the process, we have acknowledged the praxis of the Spirit of Christ in several settings and epochs, witnessing some uses and misuses of the (experience of the) Spirit in the theological arena. The Spirit has a rhetoric, a *pneumaloquence*, expressed in human experience as love, joy, and hope, and materialized as *inclusion, community,* and Christ-shaped *transmissible* practices.

The Pentecost Story and cruciformity belong to each other. Cruciformity is the *visible* side of the Pentecost experience (Acts 1:8). If we merely focus on the Pentecost experience and locate ourselves (life, thought, practice, mission) in the *created* invisible we fall into *sensationalism, inauthentic mysticism, unsituated spirituality* and become only energized as we experience the supra-human. As such, we live, literally, in "another world." In this condition, we are, using Weil's language, infinitely distant from the concrete and historical. If, on the other hand, we merely focus on the cross as the practice of Christianity, and locate ourselves in the *created* visible we fall into *anthropologism, historicalism, humanism, or dried spirituality.* In this condition, we are infinitely close to the human yet detached from the Spirit.

We are to live symbiotically as a Pentecost-shaped cruciform community. As we have commented, cruciformity is living *lo cotidiano* in dynamic correspondence with the Pentecost Story. Cruciformity is living life subversively and domestically in culture.

Latino/a theology has been given the unique historical-theological opportunity to see and tell the Story of the Spirit in culture. This praxis is beyond denominational domains for it points to the origin and continuity of Christianity, itself, in the most concrete, historical, and domestic form, *culture.* The church is God's chosen agent of transformation, the transformational parlance manifesting God's *pneumaloquence.* God's transformational rhetoric is *present* and is *presence,* in the practice of Christ peace amidst culture and history.

What now remains to be seen, however, is *how* these cultural, theological, and biblical *trajectories* appeal to life as lived by the Latino/a people of the United States and their various ecclesiological expressions? What would a Latino/a theology of the Spirit look like? Even more significant is the venture of imagining a postmodern ecclesiology in a *Latino/a way.* We undertake these challenges in the next and final chapter with difficulty and hope.

4

The Mestizo/a Community of Mañana: Imagining a Latino/a Postmodern Ecclesiology

In our previous chapter, we wrote of living in the *era of the Spirit*. In correspondence to such an era, we began to envision a theology of the Spirit with a critical *postmodern* ecclesiology. Hence, we embraced Pentecost and the cross as formative biblical narratives for the Christian experience and the process of church-making. Several theological implications emerged as result of this view. One, the Pentecost Story appears to be God's chosen narrative for authoring Christian experience. Two, the nature of the Christian community is one of continuous emergence, diversity, and heterogeneity. Three, the cross represents more than a political artifact mediating the physical execution of Jesus of Nazareth. It points to a devotion and paradigm of life. The Cross is connected to Pentecost in a symbiotic way. It represents the ethical-*visible* side of the Pentecost experience. This symbiosis reveals on one side the character of Christ in daily living as cruciformity. The cruciform life, on the other hand, is sustained by Pentecost experience (*dunamis, charismata*), which is a God-given power to live cruciformically. We concluded by identifying the church as the communal transformational parlance in and through which God's *pnemaloquence* continues to seduce and transform un-redeemed culture. Put differently, the Christian community of the Spirit represents resurrected culture (within culture), the very place of God's self-revelation and renewal.

In the present chapter, we will attempt to capitalize on both the cultural and biblico-theological developments we sought to produce in chapters two and three. Accordingly, having expanded the classical Latino/a theological use of culture to include the transcendent presence of the Spirit of Christ and having understood the church as the cruciform community of the Spirit—the communal transformational parlance of God—we now move toward the elaboration of a *Latino/a theology of the Spirit*. A *Latino/a theology of the Spirit*, we contend, is a critical discourse that views the Latino/a church as intra-cultural communities reflecting Christopraxis, that is, *Eucharistic praxis, proclamatory praxis, and pastoral praxis*.

We will proceed by presenting *Latino/a theology of the Spirit* as an ecclesiological critical discourse, alerting the theological community in general of the political and theological dangers of seeing culture as a homogeneous category when producing theological discourse. Then, we move forward to constructing Latino/a ecclesiology with three theological and cultural categories: *mestizaje, accompaniment*, and *mañana* eschatology. The finished product is a perspective of the church in a full-blooded Latino/a fashion, that is, *mestizo/a communities of mañana*. This is the Latino/a ecclesiological version of Christian communities of the Spirit, a concept we have advanced throughout our work. We will conclude this chapter by suggesting that *community organizing* is an illustration of an ecclesial praxis based on Christopraxis. In this way, we hope to show how Latino/a theology as *a practical theology of the Spirit* is capable of transforming aspects of every day life within Latino/a communities.

Latino/a Theology of the Spirit as an Ecclesial Critical Discourse

We have discussed before the relevance of liberationist methodologies for Latino/a theology (ch. 1). *Latino/a theology of the Spirit*, however, acknowledges certain limitations of liberationist methodologies, however noble and committed their attempts toward economic-political liberation. A *Latino/a theology of the Spirit* sees the nature and consequences of sin—both personal and structural—as too serious to be overcome on anthropological grounds alone. Although welcoming liberationists' claim that solution rests on the right praxis or *orthopraxis, Latino/a theology of the Spirit* asserts that such a praxis is embodied in the praxis of Jesus Christ in and through his body. Besides, *Latino/a theology of the Spirit* acknowledges that Christ's praxis did not end with Christ ascending to the heavens (Acts 1), but that his praxis has succeeded in history and culture through his Spirit in and through the church. Christ's praxis or *Christopraxis* is, then, the preferred mode of revelation-in-action for *Latino/a theology of the Spirit*. We reaffirm, therefore, that if Latino/a theology is to transform Latino/a communities, then Latino/a theology must become a critical discourse that discloses a cultural praxis that witnesses to Jesus. This claim represents the hub of all our perspectives.

Latino/a theologians, both *founders* and *builders*, have done a groundbreaking work so that emerging theologians (such as *shapers*) can paint and decorate an ecclesiological paradigm capable of embracing the heterogeneity and fluidity of cultural life and the inventive power of God's Spirit. Because of the contributions that *founders, builders, and shapers* have produced we can now imagine Latino/a churches as *cruciform communities of the Spirit* or—to say it in the Latino/a sense— *mestizo/a communities of mañana*. Our work is indeed in the direction of *painting* an ecclesiological expression that reveals Christian communities as cultural agents of the Spirit with the mission of renewing cultural life. A *Latino/a theology of the Spirit* does just that, it prepares the canvas on which Latino/a communities of the Spirit are to be imagined and appreciated. In this sense, the church is the aesthetic community of the Spirit, a source of beauty in sorrow and empowerment in struggle. The Holy Spirit is the central figure in making both: revelation and community, beauty and empowerment a concrete reality.

In the same way, we suggest that the understanding of the church as a cruciform community of the Spirit—the Pentecost-shaped resurrected culture—is the biblical-theological foundation upon which a *Latino/a* ecclesiology is to be construed. A *Latino/a theology of the Spirit* views the church as intracultural communities reflecting the praxis of the Spirit. The praxis of the Spirit—Christopraxis—is fundamentally ecclesial praxis. This ecclesial praxis, as we have suggested, is the result of two biblical images that permeates the praxis of Jesus Christ: the cross and Pentecost. The former points to cruciformity, which is living life according to the cross as an ethical demand that discloses empathic discipleship and cultural survival. The latter refers to living life according to the Spirit, a Pentecost-empowered life in community. We suggest that the preferred Latino/a ecclesial praxis is a consequence of the symbiosis of these two biblical narratives and socio-cultural paradigms.

Fundamentaly, this ecclesial praxis has a grammar and metaphysics. The grammar or rhetoric of this praxis is found in the confession, "Jesus Lord," and the metaphysics is found in the cultural practice of

"Christ's peace." The grammar is the rhetoric of the Pentecost Story, which persuades us by love, inclusion, polyphony, and affirmation of the *created* invisible realm of Christian experience. The metaphysics is the *visible* aspect of the language of God, the *pneumaloquence*—living according to the cross, in cruciformity. At the juncture of these realities we exist in real time and history as cultural creatures of the Spirit with the mission of practicing divine peace, Christ's life praxis, Christ's life project. Christopraxis, in this sense, is the practice of divine peace in the *form* of inclusion, community, and futurity. Or, as we will show the praxis of the *mestizo/a community of mañana* is a eucharistic practice, proclamatory practice, and pastoral practice.

Toward a Postmodern Theological Methodology

Methodologically and operationally speaking, *Latino/a theology of the Spirit* seems three-dimensional. On one plane, a Latino/a theology of the Spirit is a *constructive* exercise or discipline dedicated to emerge again and again as a critical-ecclesiastical apparatus that interacts with theological partners in biblical studies, history, cultural studies, social sciences, philosophy, quantum theory, and so on. In this sense, a Latino/a theology of the Spirit is to maintain an inner logic resulting from the dialectic between theory and practice. Looked at on another plane, a Latino/a theology of the Spirit is to maintain its *grassroots* connection with people's domestic life struggles and hopes. Herein, a Latino/a theology of the Spirit is parasitic to cultural life.[1] In its effort at learning and constructing domestic metaphors that enhance communal life a Latino/a theology of the Spirit must dispose of professional theological jargon and live at a vernacular (theological) rank. Yet looked at on a third plane, a Latino/a theology of the Spirit is to be conceived as the gracious work of *God's Spirit*, who produces in the Christian community a language beyond human reason, highly relational, and yet reachable by the human spirit and uncomprehensibly domestic—spirituality.[2]

1. See ch. 2 and the discussion of Tanner's view of the postmodern theological task. See also Tanner, *Theories of Culture*, 113.

2. An appreciative view of Postmodernity with regard to the gospel and spirituality in terms of interrelationality and the social-communal postmodern emphasis is offered by Grentz and Loder, see Grenz, *A Primer on Postmodernism*, and Loder, *The Logic of the Spirit*. Another interesting discussion on this topic is offered by Leonardo Boff, *La Crisis como Oportunidad de Crecimiento*.

In the present work, we have only begun to draw the initial lines and identify important coordinates of these planes. While a more localized methodology is desirable, a more comprehensive graphic of a Latino/a theology of the Spirit within these planes is prohibited given the preliminary scope of our work. A common intersection, however, is visible and clear to our methodological understanding, a Latino/a theology of the Spirit is to be a discipline that resides at the juncture of the Spirit and culture, where the Pentecost and the cross meet. As such, a Latino/a theology of the Spirit is not affixed to a universalizing and passive core or matrix, be that a tradition, history, religion, culture, anthropology, philosophy, politics, and so on. In this methodological sense, a Latino/a theology of the Spirit joins with *diaspora theology* in complying with the postmodern crisis of having to deal with "a multitude of realities" which are regarded in their individuation as "fluid, polyvalent, and polyglot: ultimately and inextricably related, implicitly or explicitly, to the various constitutive factors of social location and human identity."[3] We only add to this description of "diaspora theology" the perception that "such inextricably relatedness" in any Christian theology is to be mediated by the Spirit of the resurrected Christ—the divine cultural subject that objectifies revelation.

Perhaps the character of a Latino/a theology of the Spirit is like that of meteorology where scientists form teams committed to meet nature in its raw and most cruel climatic manifestation, storms. Teams of "storm chasers" engage with nature to experience, discern, and design creative ways to meet challenges for the sake of preserving civilization, sometimes at the expenses of their own lives. Perhaps, those (theologians or not) who dare to go after the Spirit's stormy manifestation in human history can be best called "Spirit chasers." Jesus himself seems to have related to such a methodology when confronting his religious generation:

> When you see a cloud rising in the west, you immediately say, "It is going to rain"; and so it happens. And when you see the south wind blowing, you say, "There will be scorching heat"; and it happens. You hypocrites! You know how to interpret the appearance of earth and sky, but why do you not know how to interpret the present time? And why do you not judge for yourselves what is right? (Luke 12:54–57)

3. Segovia, "In the World but Not of It," 198.

Following Jesus' advice, then, a Latino/a theology of the Spirit is to seek, discern, and design theological discourse based on its encounter with the Spirit in human culture. Hence, it is a theology appreciative of and attentive to the multiple matrixes and intersections of the Spirit with cultures. We believe that the biblical narrative of Pentecost is precisely a formative focal point of the intersection of the Spirit and human culture, revealing a multiplicity of experiences. These Pentecost-initiated experiences encompass a polyphonic witnessing to Jesus Christ and prompt an empowering ecclesial praxis that builds identity, community, and cultural renewal.

Walking away from the Homogeneous Perception of Culture

A *Latino/a theology of the Spirit* methodology represents not only "a walk toward postmodernism" but also a "walk away from" significant aspects of modern theological (dominant) discourse. For instance, the classic Niebuhrian view of *Christ and Culture*, which assumes either a cultural tension or assimilation between two homogeneous social compounds, namely, church and society, does not suffice for a Latino/a ecclesiastical concept of reality.[4] Therefore, an informed ecclesiology from the *Latino/a theology of the Spirit* perspective should begin its critical reflection by asking *where is Jesus in Latino/a culture?* The very act of asking such a question presupposes two viewpoints we have been promoting throughout our work: 1) theology is always done from a particular context and cultural perspective; 2) a critical ecclesiology must resist the temptation to view culture as a homogeneous, internally-consistent, and self-contained complex whole. The French historian and social scientist Serge Gruzinski captures our suspicions, on the latter, in an unerring style:

> It is easier to think that "everything which appears ambiguous is only apparently so, that ambiguity does not exist." The simplicity of dualistic Manichaean approaches is appealing, and when they dress themselves in the rhetoric of the otherness, they

4. John Yoder presents an excellent critique of how Richard Niebuhr uses culture in a monolithic and homogeneous way in his work *Christ and Culture*, hence a view of two different realities, namely the church and culture, generates either tension or assimilation between both. See Stassen, Yeager, Yoder, and Niebuhr, *Authentic Transformation*, 31–90.

soothe our consciences even as they satisfy our thirst for purity, innocence, and archaism.[5]

Gruzinski reminds us that the *idea* of a homogeneous and pure culture, society, or Christendom has been, in many instances, a political artifact utilized to control the soul and cultural domains of peoples and civilizations through the centuries. We judge it dangerous for theologizing, and not politically naïve, to understand the church to be "the reign of the homogeneous, the univocal, orthodoxy, sameness, the center of the world,"[6] as we have seen reflected in much of our Christian literature and in the Christianization of the world. The devastating historical consequences of theologizing with this *modus operandi* has been articulated, rather extensively, by liberation and Latino/a theologians,[7] who have denounced the futility and colonizing implications of the idea of "one true culture, one true Church, one universal history," one universal *oikoumené*, as Mendieta puts it.[8] "Now more than ever," concludes the Latino social science researcher Manuel Vásquez, "the picture of U.S. Latinos as fairly homogeneous, Catholic, Spanish-speaking urban population is misleading."[9]

The Theological Significance of Culture as Embodiment, Relationality, and Transmission

Throughout the present work, we have attempted to present culture in a different way. We have offered a vision of culture as that which in practice associates us and dissociates us from peoples and communities making possible the transmission of forms of life from generation to generation. The importance of this meaning for theologizing, we have said, rests on the fact that culture appears to be the most primal and formative-socializing matrix of human life. The categories we deemed

5. Gruzinski, *The Mestizo Mind*, 22.

6. Mendieta, "From Christendom to Polycentric Oikoumené," 74.

7. See for instance González, *Out of Every Tribe and Nation*, 31–37.

8. Mendieta contrasts the universal (monocentric) *oikoumené*—a tendency of modernism—with a polycentric *oikoumené*— a postmodern understanding—already present in liberation theologizing. In this sense, Mendieta contends, liberation theologies integrated postmodern categories in their theologizing way before postmodern theologies became available. See Mendieta, "From Christendom to Polycentric Oikoumené."

9. Vásquez, "Rethinking Mestizaje," 135.

as binding for theological production were embodiment, relationality, and transmission. In other words, we suggest that a matter is cultural if it can be embodied in practices, is relational, and can be perpetuated over time. Culture represents human embodiment as well as mobility for the perpetuation of religious forms of life. Accordingly, the church as resurrected culture is to be perceived as a privileged source for theological inquiry and revelation. In this sense, the church encompasses multiple *matrices* and *intersections* of revealed embodiments. For instance, we could think of tradition (e.g., Judaism and Christianity), biblical narrative, liturgy, the sacraments, worship, proclamation, the charismatic manifestations of the Spirit, Christopraxis, and so on.

The Latino/a Church as the *Mestizo/a Community of Mañana*

So far we have identified a *Latino/a theology of the Spirit* as a constructive and critical discourse of the church. Such a discourse has the task of imagining and constructing the *rostro* (shape) of the Latino/a church. Given the cultural fluidity distinguishing Latino/a communities and the theological categories we have gathered to engage the challenges of a postmodern context, we dare to imagine the Latino/a church as a community that under the power of the Spirit represents a socio-cultural space for survival, service, and renewal—a cultural geography we call the *mestizo/a community of mañana*.

Mestizaje as a Matrix for Christian Identity

We have suggested before that through the optic lens of the Pentecost narrative, the church is a polyphonic, heterogeneous, and emerging community. All these categories suggest that *mestizaje* is an appropriate metaphorical *intersection* or *matrix* to conceive the identity of the Christian community.

Mestizaje language may have different connotations depending on the context, cultural experience, and agenda of the interpreter. As far as we are concerned, *mestizaje* represents a hub of dehumanizing stories and self-empowering templates, particularly in the case of Latin America and the U.S. Hence, *mestizaje* represents for Latino/a theology of the Spirit an associative cultural *factor* and privileged cultural *intersection* for understanding Latino/a identity and Christian identity in general.

Some argue that *mestizaje*, in spite of its unfashionable use as a colonizing mechanism, is a very contemporary phenomenon. *Mestizaje* is becoming, argues Gruzinski, a "planetwide idiom."[10] On the one hand, *Mestizaje* seems to disclose a *globalizing* tendency; while on the other hand, it discloses a *localizing* dynamic. The former points toward decentralization, extension, fluidity, and colonization. The latter, however, points toward uniformity, affirmation of the self, and localization.[11] Next to the term *mestizaje* other cultural idioms such as *mulatez, mélange*, and *hybrid* are emerging and producing a language that points to a different way of perceiving the human self, society, economy, art, community, theology, politics, and the church.

In an attempt to describe the phenomenon of *mestizaje*, Gruzinski speaks of the *mestizo/a* effect as "[m]ixing, mingling, blending, crossbreeding, combining, superimposing, juxtaposing, interposing, imbricating, fusing, and merging." *Mulatez* is a popular concept among Latin American Caribbean areas meaning "a mixture of black (African) with white (Latin American)." In a sense it pairs with the concept of *Mélange* more than *mestizaje*. Mélange takes the connotation of the "mixing pure colors" and shifting from the "homogeneous into the heterogeneous."[12] For the purpose of our discussion, we use *mestizaje* as encompassing these other concepts.

It was the Mexican anthropologist Gonzalo Aguirre Beltrán, notices Gruzinski, who first "linked *mestizo/a* processes to acculturation." So Gruzinski entertains Aguirre Beltrán's view of mestizaje as follows:

> [*Mestizo/a* phenomena are the result of] the struggle between colonial European culture and indigenous culture . . . Opposing elements of the cultures in contact tend to be mutually exclusive, confronting and opposing each other; but at the same time they tend to interpenetrate, combining and identifying with each other.[13]

10. See Gruzinski, *The Mestizo Mind*, 17.

11. Ibid.

12. Ibid., 19.

13. Quoted in ibid., 21. See also Beltrán, *El Proceso de Aculturación*.

Gruzinski perceives that "[i]t is this very confrontation which per-
mitted the emergence of a new culture—the *mestizo/a* or Mexican
culture—born of the interpretation and combination of opposites."
Similar cultural conclusions in contexts such as Brazil suggest that
"the fluid and dynamic nature, the constant evolution, of the various
indigenous and *mestizo/a* realities" is an ongoing phenomenon.[14] On
these bases, Gruzinski argues that cultural identity does not presuppose
"an unchanging core" behind culture or a "stable, unchanging cultural
substrate."[15] For him, "every human being is endowed with a series of
identities that can be successively or simultaneously brought into play,
depending on context." Socially speaking, we are a "galaxy of individuals, each having multiple identities."[16]

Mestizaje and its processes "belong to a class of objects," commends Gruzinski, "that leave historians disarmed." He is referring here
to "clouds" which are complex, fuzzy, changing, fluctuating, ever-mov-
ing forms.[17] Following this "cloud logic," Gruzinski denies any idea of
religion (or else) as the "underlying model—universal and timeless—
composed of identical reference points independent of period, region,
or society."[18] Instead, "complexity, unpredictability, and randomness" are
inherent to *mestizaje*.

On the basis of *mestizaje* then, how is one to understand Christian
identity? How is one to talk of the Christian church as a distinctive
community? We will offer a theological response to this matter, articulating our *Latino/a theology of the Spirit*.

MESTIZAJE IN THE PENTECOST STORY

We have already articulated a Pentecost-based theology of the church
in a previous chapter. In such a theological vision, the conception of the
church as the heterogeneous and polyphonic community of the Spirit,
in our judgment, offers a proper approach to addressing Christian
identity biblically and yet from a postmodern perspective.[19] From a

14. Ibid., 22.
15. Ibid.
16. Ibid., 26.
17. Ibid., 30.
18. Ibid., 26.
19. A similar argument could be sustained from the perspective of popular Latino/a
Catholicism. For instance, Elizondo sees Virgin *Guadalupe* as a primal icon of *mestizaje*

Pentecost-based theological perspective, the Christian community is a cultural space where multiple matrixes of identities find commonality and affirmation in the Spirit of Christ, as the transcendent socializing-formative agent.[20] The Spirit as the *transcendent cultural subject* meets, we think, Gruzinski's claim that "any attempt to find cultural identity in terms of *mestizaje* will have to face the cloud model [which] supposes that all reality includes an unknowable element and that it also contains a dose of uncertainty and randomness."[21] So what is "disarming and impossible" for the social historian, becomes challenging and demanding, yet not impossible, for the *Latino/a theologian of the Spirit*. In the end, the *Latino/a theologian of the Spirit* is used to facing "clouds" in *stormy* ways.

The book of Acts offers us a view of the historical genesis of the Christian community in terms of *mestizaje*, diversity, and polyphony:

> All of them were filled with the Holy Spirit and began to speak in other languages, as the Spirit gave them ability. Now there were devout Jews from every nation under heaven living in Jerusalem. And at this sound the crowd gathered and was bewildered, because each one heard them speaking in the native language of each. Amazed and astonished, they asked, "Are not all these who are speaking Galileans? And how is it that we hear, each of us, in our own native language? Parthians, Medes, Elamites, and residents of Mesopotamia, Judea and Cappadocia, Pontus and Asia, Phrygia and Pamphylia, Egypt and the parts of Libya belonging to Cyrene, and visitors from Rome, both Jews and proselytes, Cretans and Arabs—in our own languages we hear them speaking about God's deeds of power." All were amazed and perplexed, saying to one another, "What does this mean?" (Acts 2:4–12)

What does this mean? is the question asked by those who experienced the polyphonic witnessing to Jesus Christ in this narrative. Addressing Christian identity in terms of fluid categories—such as diversity, multiculturality, distinctive affirmation of the cultural self, heterogeneity—both for the individual and the community is indeed a

---

for the Americas. The concept of *mestizaje* as "new creation" is rich and complies, in our judgment, with Gruzinski's demands. See Elizondo, *Guadalupe*.

20. Samuel Solivan, from a Latino/a Pentecostal perspective, provides good basis for this type of argument. See Solivan, "The Holy Spirit."

21. Gruzinski, *The Mestizo Mind*, 30.

challenging and *demanding* theological task for the theologian and the church of any epoch.[22] The Spirit, however, seems at home and takes this challenge with a peculiar familiarity. In this narrative, for instance, the Spirit moves in multiple directions simultaneously: it creates a common space for being-in-community and affirms the distinctiveness of each cultural reality through a polyphonic proclamation of Jesus. The Spirit shapes identity within community while creating commonality (unity) and while affirming the distinctive stories in their respective cultural locations. By the end of this Pentecost event, the Spirit had been able to create a sense of commonality called "koinonia," move human will toward a *new social engagement* called "baptism in the body of Christ," and form *new* socio-cultural practices distinctive to the *emerging Christian identity*:

> [T]hey were cut to the heart and said to Peter and to the other apostles, "Brothers, what should we do?" Peter said to them, "Repent, and be baptized every one of you in the name of Jesus Christ so that your sins may be forgiven; and you will receive the gift of the Holy Spirit." . . . So those who welcomed his message were baptized, and that day about three thousand persons were added. They devoted themselves to the apostles' teaching and fellowship, to the breaking of bread and the prayers. (Acts 2:37–39, 41–42)

This process reflects *mestizaje* at its best. In this sense, *mestizaje* is common to Christian experience and community. It has been so since the beginning of the church. González's comment on this matter is appropriate: "Just as the gospel cannot be separated from its plural and even confusing witness and reduced to a single, *monophonic* witness, so can it not be separated from the various cultures in which it takes flesh."[23] The *multiple witness* of Scripture (four gospels), for González, is not merely an apologetic mechanism to validate Christian faith on a rational level. It is a disclosure, a witness to the plurality of God's revelation, however confusing and chaotic it might appear.

Christian identity as *mestizaje* is an ambiguous and paradoxical experience, for it points to the re-ordering of life by the Spirit—the *transcendent cultural subject* (*renvoi*)—within an *emerging and heterogeneous community*. In discussing the meaning of Acts 2, Justo González

22. See Solivan, "The Holy Spirit," 57.

23. González, *Out of Every Tribe and Nation*, 31, emphasis added.

detects an ambiguity and names it "the disadvantage of the advantaged." González views this event (Pentecost) as one disclosing the nature of the church, but also the nature of the *non-(Pentecost) churched*. A reading of this passage suggests that all were searching for meaning but for different reasons. Some found themselves confused as they heard the *good news* in their own tongue yet did not comprehended the source and significance of it. They were experiencing the *polyphony* of the Pentecost or, in Gonzaléz's words, "a multiplicity of tongues, from which confusion results."[24] Others (those mocking the disciples) did understand (they thought) what that disruption meant, but they were equally confused. These others represent the *non-churched*. That is, they are those who are typically in control of and dominate the social order, economic means, ideologies, and other cultural domains. They render themselves as needless of being re-ordered within the womb of an *emerging heterogeneous community*. They represent the standard for high culture, the models of a socially refined lifestyle. In short, they need no community of the Spirit. Also, the *non-churched* could well represent those whose tradition, particular religious experience, or personal religiosity inform their theology beyond the *fresh* and *surprising* and *unpredictable* interaction of the Spirit of God.[25]

In sum, the Christian community, since its beginning, represents a cultural space where multiple matrices of identities find commonality and affirmation in the Spirit of Christ, as the transcendent socializing-formative agent. The Spirit acts in both directions simultaneously: it creates a common space for being-in-community and affirms the distinctiveness of each cultural reality within the whole through a polyphonic proclamation of Jesus. Commonality, in the Latino/a sense, implies *convivencia* (life together). Affirmation of diversity means both affirmation of the *person in the diverse body* and also affirmation of *diversity in* the person. These affirmative movements by the Spirit imply a great deal of empathy, relationality, and spirituality. In short, all this is only possible within community. This takes us to the second constructive component of our view of Latino/a ecclesiology: *community*. We will offer below a rather thorough discussion of the concept of *accompaniment*, arguing that accompaniment is the preferred social

24. González, *Acts*, 39.
25. Ibid., 37–43.

paradigm for understanding *being-in-community* from the perspective of a *Latino/a theology of the Spirit*. By extension, *accompaniment* represents an ecclesial paradigm for understanding *church-in-culture*.

The Latino/a Church as Accompaniment Community

COMMUNITY AND AESTHETIC PARTICIPATION

Goizueta offers an intelligent understanding of community based on the concept of inter-relationality. In community, notices Goizueta, we are intrinsically defined by our relationships with others.[26] Goizueta suggests that relationality, among Latino/a communities, is not a choice of the individual but a defining-social matrix intrinsic to his/her life within the community.[27] If the individual does not have "a strong constitutive sense of community," relational conceptualizations such as "individual-community" or "community-institution" will degenerate into false dichotomies. Thus, Goizueta points to sacramentality as a remedy to these dichotomistic perceptions of community. Put simply, the particular (i.e., individual) mediates the universal (i.e., community). By means of this sacramental view, Goizueta hopes to evade communal-individualistic categorizations inherited from the Enlightenment.

Goizueta sees himself as developing an organic anthropology. From this perspective, the life of particular individuals is contingent on the life of the community as a whole. So "[i]n an organic anthropology, each person is not a mirror reflection but a *unique refraction* of the whole."[28] Goizueta critiques individualistic views of community, particularly Protestant liberal individualism, for these have invented the individual as an *unsituated self*. By "unsituated self" Goizueta understands the modern-liberal idea of "community as a voluntary association of separated individuals."[29] From this social paradigm, relationality is only secondary and optional to the individual. The individual, then, emerges as a "self-enclosed entity."[30] Goizueta confronts this view and opts for a different social paradigm when understanding the individual

26. Goizueta, *Caminemos con Jesús*, ch. 3.

27. Ibid., 59 and 62.

28. Ibid., 76, emphasis original.

29. Ibid., 55. Goizueta builds on Wathtel, *The Poverty of Affluence*, 118.

30. Herein Goizueta is following the understanding of Robert Bellah et al. See ibid., 59–65.

in community: "The community to which I belong extends beyond me not only spatially but also temporally: that community includes my ancestors as well as my progeny and their progeny."[31] Goizueta sees communal life as *trans-generational*. This understanding of community gives him footing for a perception of the individual as a *community-situated self*. Here Goizueta resonates with contemporary psychological studies that understand Latino/a sense of peoplehood in terms of systems.[32] Hence, Goizueta seems to coincide with systemic social scientists in that systemic concepts such as family, home, and church can serve as better social paradigms for the understanding of community. These systemic concepts are key in the construction of human identity. As a result, Goizueta sees community as the social reality "giving birth to self-identity."[33] From Goizueta's anthropological perspective, the understanding of Jesus and the making of Christian identity, for instance, are acquired in the participation of religious practices within a given worshipping community. Similarly, physical symbols, rituals, stories, and the like mediate inter-relational bonds and, therefore, are useful means "to strengthening communal and individual identity."[34] Goizueta views physical religious symbols and practices as constructive factors mediating the concreteness of God in community. In other words God, an abstract concept among many Latinos/as Roman Catholics, finds concretion in communal practices that are mediated by physical items associated with the things such as the crucified Jesus, Mary, and the Virgin of Guadalupe. Thus, in Goizueta's perception, inter-relationality and physicality co-construct the knowledge and experience of God in the individual and the community. Liturgical practices such as processions, kissing the feet of the crucified Jesus, or focusing on the picture of the Virgin of Guadalupe can only be understood appropriately from a communal-organic perspective. The logic of such a perspective interprets material objects as mediating personal and communal faith. Since relationality requires participation in a given practice that evokes collective faith, rituals involving the person in a physical way are not only justified but necessary in order to experience empowerment and

---

31. Ibid., 52
32. See for instance Falicov, *Latino Families in Therapy*, 161–86.
33. Goizueta, *Caminemos con Jesús*, 53.
34. Ibid.

transformation. In a sense, Goizueta's theological reasoning represents a Latino/a Catholic practical theology in the most fundamental way.

Goizueta concludes, having participated in the Holy Week liturgical procession of San Fernando Cathedral (in San Antonio Texas), that aesthetic encounters of this type embody the domestic stories of participants generating an emphatic energy capable of empowering both, the individual and the community. These types of aesthetic encounters are, put simply, sources of social empowerment and domestic transformation. Goizueta testifies to this fact with the following words:

> In these communities, I have witnessed a type of empowerment and liberation taking place which, at least initially and explicitly, seems to have little connection to any social or political struggles. Indeed, in many cases, empowerment and liberation are not explicit goals at all. Seemingly, the only explicit goals are day-to-day survival and, especially, the affirmation of relationships as essential to that survival.[35]

In sum, relationality and physicality, in Goizueta's theological reasoning, infuse aesthetic energy to the individual and community as they participate in liturgy within the confines of popular Catholicism.

ACCOMPANIMENT AND BEING CHURCH

From the ecclesiological perspective, Goizueta's contribution can best be appreciated in his concept of *accompaniment*. *Accompaniment* is the consequence of Goizueta's understanding of community based on inter-relationality, sacramentality, and popular religiosity. For instance, when reflecting on the liturgical procession of the San Fernando Cathedral, again Goizueta asserts:

> This Jesus is one who accompanies us in our suffering and whom we, in turn, accompany in his. This Jesus is, thus, the source of our community: we are one insofar as we all accompany Jesus together. This Jesus is, consequently, the source of those communal bonds which constitute us as persons and as a people, thereby giving us the strength to confront life's vicissitudes.[36]

We believe this paragraph compiles Goizueta's threefold understanding of his concept of *accompaniment*. The phrase Jesus "accompanies us in

35. Ibid., 88.
36. Ibid., 67.

our sufferings" (and we accompany him too) refers to the *ethical-political content* of *accompaniment*. In this dimension of *accompaniment*, the "where" takes precedence over the "what" in the sense that domestic life (home, city, church) is where people are most concretely known. In the case of the Latino/a people the *where* (cultural, social, economic, and domestic locations) points to the poor (the what), therefore, a preferential (not exclusive) option for the poor is naturally a consequence of a commitment to accompany Latino/a people. However, poverty as a socio-political and economic category is not the *where* but the *what*, thus for Goizueta the process of transformation (of economic, political, social structures) is a byproduct of the process of transformation within the domestic/cultural location. In Goizueta's own words:

> God is revealed first and preferentially not in grand political projects of liberation and transformation, but in the "insignificant," everyday, common struggle for survival—though this later is always intrinsically related to the larger political and economic struggle. The most basic form of resistance against those forces . . . is the affirmation . . . of one's relationships . . . and one's life.[37]

Accompaniment or walking with the poor is placing oneself *where* the poor are by assuming the ethical-political consequences (geographically and materially) of such a life and by accompanying each other in a mutual struggle for survival. So, suffering is not merely an epistemological category but an aesthetic, physical, and domestic experience that the church must embody along with the poor.

Secondly, the phrase "this Jesus is the source of those communal bonds which constitute us as persons and as a people" refers to the *aesthetic dimension* of Goizueta's understanding of *accompaniment*. The act of *accompaniment* is an effort toward self-identity. In the process of self-discovery and self-affirmation *with the other*, the person commits his/her own self in practices that embody *sentimientos* (feelings, which in the Latino/a sense encompasses intuitive reasoning). Goizueta states:

> To love God is to love this particular person, Jesus of Nazareth.
> . . . To love Jesus of Nazareth is to physically *walk with him* on the way to Calvary, or to kiss his feet nailed to the cross; Jesus can no

37. Ibid.,195–96.

more be accompanied in the abstract than human beings can.
... To pray to God for our loved ones is to physically pin their
photograph to this particular crucifix, thereby establishing the
particular, concrete relationship which will make com-passion
(not just feeling, but "feeling *with*") possible. It is in and through
the concrete particular that the universal is encountered.[38]

Goizueta understands that when Latinos/as act with *sentimiento* they
experience *mestizaje* or empathic fusion. That is, their selves are "fused
in their actions" and their actions become very much an extension of
their own selves. In sum, the aesthetic dimension of *accompaniment*
points to the church as a source of identity. By walking *with* the other,
on equal terms, we are able to build identity. This also happens as the
church walk *with* their communities in every day life struggles.

Finally, the phrase "thereby giving us the strength to confront
life's vicissitudes" refers to the *religious dimension* of *accompaniment*.
Accompaniment for Goizueta is essentially a sacramental act, a eucharistic practice, a spiritual option. *Accompaniment* as spirituality means, for
Goizueta, the transformation of the self—the most fundamental place
where ultimately liberation is experienced. The church (an extension
of the home and the city) for Goizueta "as a place for worship derives
its significance precisely from its position between the home and the
city. The church, then, as a worship [aesthetic] space is *where* we get to
know a God for whom there are no barriers, borders, or boundaries."[39]
To worship is to *feel* at home at the crossroads of domestic life, is to "be
transformed body *and* soul."

ACCOMPANIMENT FROM THE PERSPECTIVE OF LATINO/A
THEOLOGY OF THE SPIRIT

Accompaniment as a social paradigm for understanding anthropology,
ecclesiology, and social ethics, in our judgment, represents a contribution not confined to Latino/a theology alone but to Christian theology
in general and to the field of practical theology in particular.[40]

From a classical Latino/a theological perspective, Goizueta's view
of the person as a *community-situated self* and his theory of empower-

38. Ibid., 196.

39. Ibid., 210.

40. Goizueta anticipates that *accompaniment* can become a resourceful paradigm
for Hispanic theology. See ibid., 205.

ment and transformation as result of participation in communal worship represents an *advantageous theological paradigm* in several aspects.
One, Jesus' presence in the Christian community is as concrete as the
physical and relates to us as a "compañero/a de sufrimiento" (companion in suffering). Two, aesthetics becomes *analogia relationis*, the way
to know God in the concrete. Three, the church (not the state or other
power structure) is the place of empowerment, social transformation,
and liberation. Goizueta's proposal offers an alternative model for
people's liberation. In Goizueta's transformational vision there are no
explicit programs mediated by human action or praxis, as it appears to
be in the case of liberation theologies. Empowerment, social transformation, and ultimately liberation are implicit cultural products of the
aesthetic participation in community, as the people reaffirm their identities in the praxis of (non-violent) resistance toward dominant cultural
pressures of assimilation.

That being said, we perceive some theological difficulties in
Goizueta's concept of community and *accompaniment*. We will ad-
dress these difficulties from the perspective of a *Latino/a theology of
the Spirit.*

First, Goizueta's view of sacramentality, based primarily on physical relationality and immanence (immanent sacramentality), evacuates
the understanding of *sacramentum* of any *mysterium*. As a consequence
of this we confront an epistemological limitation, the knowledge of God
is restricted to aesthetic encounters between the human and the divine
mediated (mainly) by the physical. So God is God in the physical and
the concrete, period. Thus Latinos/as relate to the physical by way of
aesthetic encounters (such as processions and liturgy) requiring a physical touch so to speak. While we concur with Goizueta in that Latinos/
as are relational beings and that aesthetic is a mode of knowledge, we
disagree in that physicality is the only way or the best way to achieve
knowledge of God and the *other*. Although the physical, the historical,
the concrete are mediums by which truth is revealed, the process of revelation itself embraces transcendence and mystery.[41] In the same breath,

41. Anderson's middle point between radical transcendence and immanence is
captured in his interpretation of Bonhoffer historical transcendence. In sum, the reality
of God is known in community as historical transcendence. Such a knowledge is not
mediated by reason but by God himself who prompts a concrete encounter (ontic)
of beings-in-mutual-relation. Communal-social relationality is what constructs, for

aesthetic encounters can be mediated as well by non-physical elements such as memories, aromas, thoughts (imagination), sounds (e.g, coritos [Latino/a hymns]), the Spirit's transcendence, and so on. In Goizueta's immanent sacramentality, however, the *transcendent* presence of God as the Incarnated Son—Jesus Christ, the primal sacrament (cf. theologies of von Balthasar, Barth, and Schillebeeckx)—seems annihilated by a popular-immanent Jesuology that takes many forms (Jesus, Mary, el sagrado corazón, etc.).[42]

The *unnecessary* veiling of the transcendence of God in *physical* immanence invites metaphysical misinterpretations, our second problem. In this regard, we see a greater advantage in the Orthodox trinitiarian understanding of transcendence by David Hart. "[T]he Christian God is at once infinitely more transcendent of and, in consequence, infinitely nearer to finite reality than was the inaccessible God of antique metaphysics" and, we add, the materialized God of physical sacramentality.[43] Authentic transcendence, for that matter, is infinite proximity to the human entity. David Hart, then, is clear that God is "being in its trancendence, free from ontic determination, wholly transcendent and immanently present."[44] Physical sacramentality, on the other hand, might suggest a divine accommodation and descent from *unity* to *plurality*, thus leaving very little distinction, if any, between the reality of God and that of ritualism, communalism, and pragmatism.

The third problem is soteriological. If, as Goizueta seems to suggest, the person is a sacrament, then *to what extent does the person need redemption and sanctification?* Fourth, we face a pneumatological and ecumenical difficulty. The neglect of the Holy Spirit in popular sacramental life not only denies the reality of a *non-physical aesthetics* but radically excludes growing Latino/a traditions such as the Roman Catholic and Protestant Charismatics, and the Pentecostals. We understand that Goizueta is doing theology from a particular location, namely Latino/a popular Catholicism as experienced in the life of San Fernando Cathedral community, although his views at times point

---

Bonhoeffer and Anderson, the proper horizon for the encounter of the human subject and God. See particularly Anderson, *Historical Transcendence and the Reality of God*, chs. 2 and 3.

42. Goizueta, *Caminemos con Jesús*, 32.

43. Hart, *The Beauty of the Infinity*, 182.

44. Ibid., 183.

beyond that. Because of that, we have difficulty seeing it as representational of Latino/a religiosity in general. Latino/a religiosity is much more diverse and complex than the context Goizueta is interacting with in *Caminemos con Jesús*. Hence, we feel compelled to recommend some modifications to Goizueta's view of community and *accompaniment*.

From the perspective of *Latino/a theology of the Spirit*, we suggest that modifications of the view of "humans as sacramental entities and community-situated selves" are recommended in the service of a more inclusive, ecumenical, biblical, and postmodern approach. Our task will begin with Karl Barth's view of the Holy Spirit as *mediator of communion*, and then particular modifications will follow.

Karl Barth presents the Spirit operationally as the shaper of life within the Christian community. For Barth, the Spirit of God is *the mediator of communion* who provides communal content *between* and *within* God and humanity.[45] According to George Hunsinger's review of Barth, *koinonia* (communion) is the work of the Holy Spirit, that is, "love in knowledge, and knowledge in love, thus fellowship and mutual self-giving."[46] The making of community is indeed a task of the divine community thus encompasing a trinitarian dynamic. Authentic communion with Christ, with the trinity, and with one another, for Barth, is impossible on anthropological grounds, thus the need for the *mediatior of communion*, the Holy Spirit. In this line of thought, therefore, it is consistent to understand the Holy Spirit as the *maker of the Christian fellowship*. In other words, the Spirit is the *socializing* divine factor bringing concretion and authenticity to Christian life. In this regard, Hunsinger's comment on Barth is in order:

> The community "does not lead to any independent life in relation to its members. It lives in them." The community gathered by the Spirit is a true fellowship, not "a collective in whose existence . . . the individual is not required as such," . . . The union of the believers is firm, "but it is union in freedom."[47]

---

45. Our brief exposition of Barth's doctrine of the Spirit depends, in part, on Hunsinger's review of Barth's view of the Spirit. See Hunsinger, *Disruptive Grace*, 148–85.

46. Ibid., 151.

47. Ibid., 172.

The Holy Spirit prepares the person to experience true fellowship. Koinonia once achieved (e.g., initiated by the Spirit's baptism)[48] means *existence in communion* with God and with each other as mediated by the Holy Spirit and not by any other means (e.g., liturgy, knowledge, works, etc). Thus, for Barth the Spirit is not a variable in the process of *community-making*, it is a constant.[49]

Based on our perception of Barth's view of the Holy Spirit as *mediator of communion* and Goizueta's immanent sacramentality, we suggest that both views can be reconciled and become complements. On the one hand, Goizueta's immanent sacramentality assumes that God is already present in the human entity and that God's content is at our own disposal. That is, we can enact God's content as revelation (in us) through the physical participation in religious practices, within the context of community and worship. On the other hand, Barth acknowledges the fact that every person is a sinner and as such lives in contradiction to his/her God-given nature.[50] In such a condition, no person is in herself/himself capable of enacting God's self-revelation upon himself/herself, thus the need of a redeemer—Jesus Christ. Jesus Christ is indeed the primal sacrament of God fully disclosing who God is and who human beings are. The Spirit of Jesus is operationally the Holy Spirit, who perpetuates the primal sacramental role of Jesus Christ as the *mediator of communion*.

We suggest that Goizueta's view should include the Holy Spirit as the primal sacramental presence and primal *mediator of communion*. That is, the Holy Spirit is Christ transcendent sacrament in community (cf. Romans 8:9ff). In addition, we suggest that Goizueta's organic anthropology should incorporate the Holy Spirit as *the formative-socializ-*

48. On this matter, Barth's discussion on the Spirit revolves in how the Spirit prepares us to embrace Christian life in its fullness. Spirit's baptism is part of such a process. See Barth, *Church Dogmatics,* Vol. IV, Part 1, 650–725.

49. We acknowledge the fact that a similar discussion can be traced among Roman Catholic circles especially after Vatican II and ecclesial documents such as *Lumen Gentium.* It is understood that Catholic theologians such as Yves Congar (*The Word and the Spirit*), Heribert Mühlen (*Una Mystica Persona*), and Karl Rahner (*Experience of the Spirit*) have taken the doctrine of the Spirit within the Roman Catholic tradition to another level; one that points to the Spirit as the sustainer and shaper of the Christian community. We became aware of this fact through the work of Kärkkäinen. See Kärkkäinen. *Pneumatology.*

50. See Barth, *Church Dogmatics,* Vol. III, Part 2, 205–222.

ing factor of the self. The Holy Spirit belongs to the human soul and the soul to the Spirit as *compañero/a del alma* (companion of the soul). The Spirit relational operation concentrates on reconstructing the image of God in the individual and the community, by means of a Spirit-to-spirit interrelationality.[51] From the Christian perspective, then, we should think of: *regenerated self-in-community* instead of a *community-situated self.*

After these suggestions, we believe Goizueta could still develop his views within the sphere of popular Catholicism. Many influential Catholic theologians have indeed embraced a view of the Christian community as "the work of the Spirit."[52] For instance, Spirit-regenerated Latinos/as can now enact God's self disclosure upon themselves as they participate in community and in worship. Physical objects, religious practices, and biblical narratives can enhance and stimulate spirituality, for the Holy Spirit is active within the self of the individual and the community and operates assisting the person in the appropriation of meaning (God's knowledge) while physically participating in liturgical practices. As a matter of fact, the historical transcendence of the Holy Spirit as the *mediator of communion* might strengthen Goizueta's claim that participation in worship and community brings empowerment and liberation to the individual and the community. In this sense, the person and the community (church) are potentially sacramental expressions of the primal sacrament, the Spirit of Christ.

Another benefit of our modified view is that Latino/a charismatic communities within both Roman Catholicism and Protestantism are included in such a theological perspective and may become more enthusiastic to seek in *accompaniment,* basis for their ecclesiological understanding.

With this fundamental modification in mind, we believe that *accompaniment* is the preferred social paradigm for understanding

---

51. Loder has advanced a persuasive argument in favor of the existence of the human spirit in inter-relationality with the Spirit of God. He brings out new neuropsychological data and puts it in a theological perspective in order to argue in favor of such inter-relationality. See Loder, *The Logic of the Spirit,* 10–15. From a Latino/a perspective, both Elizabeth Conde-Frazier and Samuel Solivan recognize the relational connection between the human spirit and God's Spirit, particularly when acquiring epistemic (cognitive and aesthetic) knowledge of God. See Rodríguez and Martell-Otero, eds., *Teologia En Conjunto,* chs. 4 and 5.

52. See Sachs, "'Do Not Stifle the Spirit.'"

Latino/a ecclesiology. *Accompaniment*, as we have suggested, is intrinsic to the personhood and mediation of the Holy Spirit with regard to the Christian community. First of all, *accompaniment* is the sacramental presence of God as Spirit in the Pentecost—experienced concretely as *mestizaje*, community, and historical transcendence. Second, the Pentecost points to the "yes" of God in culture and reveals Jesus Christ as the God who continues to walk *with* his people, giving them, identity, affirmation, and empowerment. Third, cruciformity is *accompaniment* in a radical and ethical way. Cruciformity expresses the commitment to walk on multiple geographies and dimensions simultaneously: walking *as* Christ's eucharistic *mestizo* body (inclusion), walking within culture as a *proclamation* (saving) community, and walking with the world as a *pastoral* (serving) community.

In sum, from the perspective of Latino/a theology of the Spirit *accompaniment* is paradigmatic in two ways: it serves as a social paradigm to understanding *convivencia* (being-in-community) and represents an *ecclesial paradigm* for the understanding of the church-in-culture. We will turn next to see how the Latino/a *church-in-culture* is imagined as resurrected culture, as *mañana* culture. This is the third and final aspect of our ecclesiological construction.

Latino/a Church as the Embodiment of Mañana Vision and Spirit

So far we have imagined the Latino/a church as a socio-cultural territory revealing two attributes: a *mestizo/a* identity and a *communal self* known as *accompaniment*. As such, the *mestizo/a* community of the Spirit is a crossway of paradoxes and ambiguities. On the one hand, the *mestizo/a* body of Christ is a hub of *mixing* with the oppressor and cohabitating with the exploiter. On the other hand it is a place of self-*discovery*, of being enriched by the fluidity of *other* cultural identities, of encountering a *common intersection* for surviving, hoping, and believing in the possibility of a better future. The practice of every day life in such a chaotic borderline existence, we believe, is only possible under the *aleteo del Espíritu* (fluttering of the Spirit). *Mañana* is essentially an eschatological understanding of the church based on the Spirit of Christ in historical perspective. As far as we are concerned, *Mañana* is the story of the *mestizo/a community* of Christ moving *toward* God's promised future *in* today's challenging context *by* the *aleteo del Espíritu*.

Latinos/as practice every day life in a rather particular way. Maldonado reminds us what it is to be a member of the Latino/a community:

> [T]o experience life as a member of the *mestizo/a/*mulato population, which understands its birth in the context and outcome of the conquest and which has experienced oppression and colonialization throughout its history and continues today to identify with the poor and the oppressed.[53]

Maldonado points to the fact that poverty, marginalization, and oppression, among other realities, are historical forces shaping Latino/a 'culture worlds' in the U.S. context. The transnational lifestyle expressed in the social flux that results from continuous Latin American immigration as well as the emerging forms of Latino/a cultural items such as music, art, communal violence (gangs), popular religious rituals, and so on, are an evidence of life being constructed amidst such a chaotic, diverse, and resisting environment. Hence, *Mañana* becomes a very relevant Latino/a theological concept in this respect.[54]

Mañana Vision

Mañana, which translates into the English as "tomorrow," is really an eschatological notion developed from the perspective of the Holy Spirit.[55] Interestingly, Justo González develops this understanding as he explores the Pauline notion of what it means to be spiritual. Gonzaléz resists the dichotomy "spirit-matter." He finds that Paul's understanding of "being spiritual" does not result in an anti-thesis to "matter" but to the "old nature." Consequently, being spiritual has to do with having a *new life* and experiencing the power of the *Spirit*, who "intervenes to make things become what they are not."[56] González then factors the view of the (Latino/a) church in function of the reality of the triune God:

---

53. Maldonado, "Doing Theology and the Anthropological Questions," 110.

54. See González, *Mañana*.

55. For an eschatological utilization of González's concept of *mañana* see Pedraja, *Teología*, 187–204. and Escobar, *Changing Tides*, 147–49.

56. González, *Mañana*, 160.

> For Hispanics, the church is a pilgrim people, but a people whose pilgrimage is no uncertain wandering. It is pilgrimage to a *mañana* made possible by the dead and resurrection of Jesus Christ, made present by the power of the Spirit, and made certain by the power and promise of none other than God Almighty.[57]

Latino/a theology of the Spirit is sympathetic with this understanding. Further, *mañana thought* as an eschatological category provides the basis for seeing Latino/a churches as resurrected culture or *mañana culture*.

The Latino/a theologian Luis Pedraja capitalizes creatively on the eschatological notion of *mañana* in his work, *Teología*. Pedraja's theological interactions are welcome into our ecclesiological construction, particularly with regard to three items: creation, resurrection, and his eschatological maxim. In correspondence with these, we will introduce three concepts: *mañana thought, mañana talk,* and *mañana walk*. These are domestic concepts reflecting surviving, hoping, and believing *latinamente*.

Mañana Thought—Creation and Radical Living

Mañana, expresses Pedraja, is about "a radical hope that the future will be transformed to bring justice, liberation, and life."[58] Consequently, *mañana* should be understood as a radical questioning of the present by the future as envisioned by God. Pedraja detects a principle that guides his *mañana* theologizing. We call this principle *mañana thought*—one that judges the present and calls for its transformation (in God's terms).[59] Creation is perceived, according to *mañana thought*, as an affirmation of the current existence and the possibility of the *new* created order in the *now*—the possibility of God actualizing his promises in our midst. Latinos/as, notices Pedraja, tend to see creation in a sacred fashion. This fact, we believe, precipitates Latinos/as for celebrating life in *lo cotidiano* (every day life) with hope. Further, this way of conceiving the created natural order brings about in Latinos/as a sense of survival. In this sense, creation points to survival, and survival to *mañana* living. *Mañana*

---

57. Ibid., 166–67.
58. Pedraja, *Teología*, 188.
59. Ibid.

living is radical living, that is, the practice of life against the oath of re-
sisting-oppressive environments. *Mañana living*, in the Latino/a sense,
is surviving because, somehow, God wants us to.

Mañana Talk—Radical Hope

A *mañana* theologian does not fear resurrection as part of his/her
discourse—as tends to be the case in many academic settings, where
the resurrection is disregarded as non-historical. *Mañana* implies going to bed knowing that I will wake up tomorrow morning to keep on
going with life—*mañana sera otro día* (tomorrow will be another day).
Latino/a people are *mañana-friendly people*. So preachers, priests, and
theologians dealing with Latino/a communities do not typically fear
addressing them in *mañana* tones. Resurrection is intrinsic to *mañana*
talk. There are many sayings among Latinos/as which point to that
fact.

The familiar saying *mañana sera otro día* is an affirmation that
there is a life tomorrow. It shows a commitment to deal with life as it
is, to adapt, to design, to construct life even beyond systems, structures,
and traditions. There is a sense, among Latinos/as that *siempre hay un
mañana* (there is always a tomorrow). These Spanish adages are popular
domestic items constituting, in our opinion, cultural pericopes. That being the case, *mañana talk* has been around for a while among Latinos/
as. Particularly among many Protestant Latino/a churches, *mañana talk*
is resourceful. Many Christian denominations in the United States are
used to the task of manufacturing programs, initiatives, ministries, and
educational apparatuses for Latino/a pastors and churches while excluding Latino/a leaders at the planning phase. However, after everything
has been settled in a non-Latino/a way, these religious establishments
expect Latino/a pastors and ministries to succeed. But a worse approach
is when such denominations do not see the need to include—not even a
caricature of—Latino/a communities in their ministerial configuration
even when their immediate demographic context is Latino/a. In spite
of these circumstances, many Latino/a Christian leaders and churches
manage to survive and even outgrow dominant-culture churches. From
a new church planting perspective, *the word on the street* is that while
many dominant-culture churches and denominations are declining in
attendance (enclosed in their well-equipped facilities), many Latino/a

churches are surviving and growing without facilities, equipment, and financial means. These Latino/a churches see themselves as New-Testament-like communities led by God to make it, hope it, proclaim it. Latino/a talk is full of *mañana talk* and radical hope. It is like post-Easter or Pentecost talk.

Mañana Walk—Radical Practiced Belief

Mañana should not be understood as laziness or irresponsibility, so argues González, for *mañana* "is much more than tomorrow."[60] Pedraja appeals to a popular Spanish adage to illustrate what we call *mañana walk: que será, será* (whatever will be, will be).[61] Pedraja suggests that this phrase "is a statement of faith" rather than a fatalistic or procrastinating attitude of the Latino/a people. We concur with Pedraja, particularly from the perspective of the *mestizo/a communities* of the Spirit.

Que será, será assumes that God is immanently present in community and in daily life. From our perspective, it means that the Spirit as the historical transcendent *mediator* in community intervenes to make things become what they are not. *Que será, será* presupposes an inter-relationality with the Spirit.

Second, *Que será, será* as an expression embodied in popular songs, family exclamations, and daily choices, reveals *sentimiento* (aesthetic knowledge). This phrase points to the fact that Latinos/as invest themselves in such a confession and are fused in desirable events even before such events are actualized. In other words, they are empathically committed in any practice or action conveying to the realization of what they expect to happen. In a way, they experience *mañana* aesthetically.

Third, *Que será, será* acknowledges the Spirit as a source of possibility and creativity, of faith and hope. In this regard Pedraja hopes that "*Que será, será* might serve theology as an eschatological maxim, calling us to trust God with the future and work to make the reign of God a reality in the present."[62]

In sum, *Que será, será* far from being an irresponsible act, represents a personal or communal statement of radical belief, embodied

60. González, *Mañana*, 164.
61. Pedraja, *Teología*, 201.
62. Ibid., 202.

in cultural practices, religious rituals, family life, Christian witnessing, charismatic works of the Spirit, and so on.

Conclusions

The Latino/a church and *mañana* vision are both part of the same story, God's eschatological story of resurrection and renewal. The Latino/a church should become the embodiment of *mañana* story. *Mañana* is the story of the *mestizo/a community* of the Spirit of Christ moving *toward* God's promised future *in* today's challenging context. In this "pilgrimage toward *mañana*" the *mestizo/a community* is to *think, talk,* and *walk* in a *mañana* way. As a *mestizo/a community of mañana,* the church is a source of survival, radical hope, and radical belief. Accordingly, the church is to become a *community of survival, hope, and belief where the future will be transformed to bring justice, liberation, and life,* by the *aleteo del Espíritu.* In this way, the *mestizo/a community of mañana* is to bring about *mañana culture,* that is, a story of resurrection and renewal in the midst of cultural complexities and chaotic existence.

Practical Conclusions: Community Organizing as a Transformative Ecclesial Praxis That Witnesses to Jesus

At the beginning of the present work we quoted the missiologist Orlando Costas, one of the Latino/a theological *founders*:

> Christ transforming power is mediated by the work of the Spirit in the life and witness of the church. . . . The point, however, is not of theological precision and missiological awareness but, rather, of commitment and practice.[63]

Our entire work somehow interacted with Costas' claim by way of *commuting* from cultural (theological) anthropology to Latino/a theology, and from the Pentecost understanding of the church toward an updated concept of the Latino/a church as a *mestizo/a community of mañana.* During our *commuting,* we traveled, acknowledging the Spirit, among such challenging discourses as practical theological methodologies, Latino/a theologizing, various perceptions of culture, a Pentecost/cross-based theology, postmodern visions of communal identities, and Latino/a eschatology. We have *commuted,* however, aware of our lack

---

63. Costas, *Christ Outside the Gate,* 16.

of "theological precision" as Costas puts it, but with a commitment to signaling to the continuing praxis of Jesus Christ in today's complex cultural worlds. Jesus' historical praxis, or Christopraxis, we argued throughout our work, is the praxis of the Spirit making of the church *Jesus' resurrected culture* or *mañana* culture.

The church, from a *Latino/a theology of the Spirit* perspective, is the *mestizo/a community of mañana* and is responsible for perpetuating Jesus' historical praxis in a cultural way. The praxis of the *mestizo/a community of mañana* is to be one that constantly discloses the *intersection* of the Spirit of Christ with (Latino/a) culture in a way that (1) should create commonality and affirm distinctive cultural stories while allowing the multiple formative matrices to shape life in community under the guidance of the Spirit, (2) should enhance interrelationality among the members of a community by the Spirit mediation as the basis for being-in-community, and (3) should unleash *thought-talk-walk mañana* processes by means of which members of a community radically interrogate the present while appropriating the preferred future of God in today's domestic (urban) situation. The *mañana* theologian Justo González, again, captures our perspective of church praxis and provides us with a frame of reference:

> Because the Church is a community of the Spirit or, what is the same, a community of "the last days," part of its mission is to witness to the future that God has promised. That testimony must be given, not only in words, not merely through the individual lives of Christians, but also through the communal life of the Church. . . . It is true that modern life is very complicated, and that a simple *commonality of goods* such as is described in Acts [e.g., 4:31–33] presents enormous difficulties. But this does not free us from the need to seek *ways in which our community may be a sign* pointing toward the coming reign of God.[64]

This paradigmatic view of the church as the witnessing community of the Spirit in society urges today's church to become both biblical and yet relevant to its current social context. We will argue next that *community organizing* as an ecclesial praxis approximates González's paradigmatic view, thus offering a viable praxis for the Latino/a church in today's urban context.

---

64. González, *Acts*, 80, emphasis added.

Community Organizing: A Witness to the Future

The quote above suggests that Justo González considers "commonality of goods" to be a relevant social testimony of the New Testament church to its surrounding communities. González alleges that, although "commonality of goods" is a rather complicated social process in today's context, we as a church are responsible for finding ways to perpetuate an ecclesial testimony pointing to Jesus as the regenerator of community life. We would like to suggest that *community organizing as an ecclesial praxis* is one of these ways. We will proceed by introducing *community organizing* in a nonreligious fashion. We will later discuss the kind of *community organizing* approach we subscribe to and will build an argument in favor of the need of the church in the city to become an agent of inclusion and empowerment.

Community Organizing as a Vision of Affirmation and Empowerment for Impoverished Urban Communities

Community organizing is essentially a *praxis of social empowerment* aiming toward the betterment of community life in a given context (e.g., barrio, city, etc.). Methodologically speaking, community organizing is a *social process* based on the communal exercise of self-betterment. Community organizing employs a language constructed from within the constituency of a given community—a language that aims at social empowerment. This language, seeking to unleash the human capital of a given community, co-creates a communal inner logic for reasoning and acting in favor of the community as a whole. Such an endeavor entails finding a *shared vision of community development* that should emerge out of the constituency of a given community.

The shared vision is to encourage inclusion, participation in the planning process, and motivate participants toward imagining the preferred common future for the community. Meanwhile, the process of community organizing itself focuses on "mapping the community assets" and delineating the necessary processes to undergo for achieving such a desired life condition.[65] Community organizing entails a bipolar social process. On the one hand, there is (social) inclusion, participation, unification, and communal imagination. On the other hand, there

65. See Kretzmann and Mcknight, *Building Communities from the Inside Out*, particularly pp. 345–64.

is (socio-economic) assessment, task distribution, decentralization, and leadership development.

We accept the Kretzmann-Mcknight thesis that the most appropriate approach to achieving community development, in a devastated community, is that of an *asset-based* approach as contrasted with the traditional *needs-driven* approach. This is the preferred vision of community organizing we subscribe to in our discussion.[66]

TOWARD AN AFFIRMING AND EMPOWERING APPROACH

Kretzmann-Mcknight see that "by focusing on a community's needs, deficiencies and problems" we pollute our approach with "negative images," creating a "mental map" that guides our actions pessimistically toward the community.[67] Consequently, we end up producing deficiency-oriented policies and programs in an attempt to regenerate community life. The major flow of *needs-driven* approaches is perceivable in their vision of target communities they attempt to give assistance. These approaches, argue Kretzmann-Mcknight, foster a consumerist mentality with regard to devastated communities. Hence, communities become "consumers of services, with no incentive to be producers."[68]

We may also add to Kretzmann-Mcknight's critique that *needs-driven approaches* create an *urban side effect*. Needs-driven approaches cause devastated communities to fall into a type of *internal colony status*. They become *identifiable sub-developed neighborhoods* under the power of external policies and oppressive urban perceptions. One may recall here Mirandé's view of internal colony.[69] In essence, *internal colony* describes how a community has ceased to hold their own sociopolitical and economic power, by being forced into a political-economic-social power of another (dominant) community(s)—which tends to be oppressive in nature. For instance, in the case of Chicano/as (or Latinos/as), Mirandé observes that by the mere fact of a person speaking Spanish or being identified as a Spanish-speaking descendent, that person is placed (categorized) in an internal colony status better known as (Hispanic,

66. The seminal work of John Kretzmann and John Mcknight is assumed here. See ibid., 1–11.

67. Ibid., 1–2.

68. Ibid., 2.

69. See the discussion in ch. 1 above.

Latino/a) Chicano/a, Mexican American, etc. Although Mirandé
uses this concept from a socio-cultural and political perspective, and
applied it to Chicanismo many years ago, the concept serves us well
when applying it to devastated communities in *relation to* surrounding developed communities. A good deal of the popular *urban perception* of devastated communities is culturally and racially conditioned
in the context of the United States. For instance, the common phrases,
"that's a Mexican barrio!" or "that's a Puerto Rican ghetto!" or "that's a
Filipino neighborhood," are all statements carrying cultural and racial
connotations, generally skewed toward a *cheap-life-quality* perception.
Perceptions such as these soon become urban-cultural stereotypes that
induce negative messages of "cheap life" into impoverished communities. A *needs-driven approach*, therefore, has the effect of *disempowering*
the very community it seeks to assist. Hence, Kretzmann-Mcknight
conclude that "they [devastated communities] begin to see themselves
as people with special needs that can only be met by outsiders."[70]

The "alternative approach" as presented by Kretzmann-Mcknight
sees the community from a different angle. The very fact that there is
a community "out there" means that life is taking place in that community. It is acknowledged that in sub-developed communities life is
experienced in a rather negative and somehow detrimental way; yet,
community is alive and struggling to survive. Further, it means that
these communities have certain assets, they have potential for improv-
ing community life, and they can produce *better* forms of social life.
Kretzmann-McKnight claim, "[t]hat alternative path, very simply, leads
toward the development of policies and activities based on the capaci-
ties, skills and assets of lower income people and their neighborhoods."[71]
This appreciative approach is not *corresponding* but *hermeneutical* in
nature. That is, the key question posed to a community is not *what can
we bring into this community to make it work?* Rather, the key question
is *how is this community working and how do we create resources from
within?* Under this appreciative approach, community organizing/de-
velopment takes a different course of action:

> Key to neighborhood regeneration, then, is to locate all of
> the available local assets, to begin connecting them with one

70. Kretzmann and McKnight, *Building Communities from the Inside Out*, 2.
71. Ibid., 5.

another in ways that multiply their power and effectiveness, and
to begin harnessing local institutions that are not yet available
for local development purposes. . . . Each community boasts a
unique combination of assets upon which to build its future.
. . . Household by household, building by building, block by
block.[72]

In sum, the *appreciative approach* envisions a *community out there*
which already has an identity of its own, however confusing, disorganized, or detrimental it might appear. Second, this approach acknowledges *inter-relationality* or *inter-connectivity* as the appropriate way to produce communal life and generate transforming events.
Finally, this approach anticipates the possibility to *build a future* within
this community.

A question remains, however. Given urban communities are diverse socio-cultural bodies disclosing multiple centers for social engagement and identity formation, which communal spaces and agents
are the most influential and catalytic for the regeneration of the community as a whole? To this matter we turn next, arguing that while the
city is a vast territory of urban realities, the need of a particular type of
transforming (urban) community, namely the church, is required for
the regeneration of the whole.

The City and the Need for a New Urban Community

Seeing Manhattan from the 110th floor of the World Trade
Center. Beneath the haze stirred up by the winds, the urban is-
land, a sea in the middle of the sea, lifts up the skyscrapers over
Wall Street, sinks down at Greenwich, then rises again to the
crests of Midtown, quietly passes over Central Park and finally
undulates off into the distance beyond Harlem. . . . This gigantic
mass is immobilized before the eyes. It is transformed into a
texturology in which extremes coincide—extremes of ambition
and degradation, brutal oppositions of races and styles, contrasts between yesterday's buildings, already transformed into
trash cans, and today's urban irruptions that block out its space.
. . . New York has never learned the art of growing old by playing on all its pasts. Its present invents itself, from hour to hour,

---

72. Ibid., 5–6.

in the act of throwing away its previous accomplishments and challenging the future. . . .[73]

This vision of the city of the renowned French social scientist Michel de Certeau coincides with many experts in the fact that the city is alive. In Certeau's words it is "transformed"; "[i]ts present invents itself from hour to hour." Neighborhoods, barrios, ghettoes, suburbs, are all transforming, changing, and developing—some for good and some for bad. In this section we want to imagine these neighborhoods, barrios, and ghettoes walking with the church into *mañana* transformation.

At first hand, community organizing might suggest *doing something to (a) community*. This superficial understanding, however, was challenged by Kretzmann-McKnight as we have previously shown. Community organizing, though compiling two ideas *community* and *organization*, centers on the community. Put simply, it is enabling the community to do something for itself, to grow into a *mañana*-type of community.

A similar approach to Kretzmann-McKnight's is emerging from a rather different axis, the entrepreneurship sector. Peter F. Drucker, in the book *The Organization of the Future*, draws a historical profile of the development of the concept of "the organization." He goes back as far as the 1860s, finding that organizations were thought to be based on control, command, and ownership. In such a primitive-capitalistic setting, organizations were utilized as tools for achieving production. That perception of the organization has been changing due in part to the development of local businesses, global markets, and emerging social contexts. In our time, Drucker notices,

> The organization is, above all, *social*. It is people. Its purpose must therefore be to make the *strengths of people effective and their weaknesses irrelevant*. In fact, that is the one thing only the organization can do—the one reason why we have it and need it.[74]

In his contribution to *The Community of the Future*, Peter Drucker draws our attention to the importance of community in itself as a source of city life. He makes a case where he presents the need for a *new*

73. De Certeau, *The Practice of Everyday Life*, 91.

74. Drucker, "Introduction: Toward the New Organization," 5, first emphasis original, second emphasis added.

urban community—the only one able to alleviate the chaos experienced in the life of the city.[75] He proposes a process he calls "civilizing the city." Civilizing the city refers to the role "social-based communities" play in bringing moral equilibrium to the social life of a city. These alternative communities are of a different order than those of businesses or government. They belong to the social sector. These communities should target, in Drucker's opinion, a particular aspect of life in the city: the social. The government or the private sector of society cannot create (moral) social life in the city in order to alleviate the social chaos. Drucker outlines his view with the following words:

> Only the institution of the social sector, that is, the non-government, non-business, nonprofit organization, can create what we now need, communities for citizens and especially for the highly educated knowledge workers who, increasingly, dominate developed societies. One reason for this is that only nonprofit organizations can provide the enormous diversity of communities we need—from churches to professional associations, and from community organizations taking care of the homeless to health clubs. . . . Only the nonprofit social sector institution can provide opportunities to be a volunteer and thus can enable individuals to have both: a sphere in which they are in control and a sphere in which they can make a difference.[76]

Two observations regarding Drucker's perception of the church and society are in order: one negative and one positive. On the one hand, Drucker's perception of the church as a civilizing force posits a negative connotation on the rest of society. It can be taken as if chaos points to uncivilized people. If Drucker's idea of uncivilized people is based, for instance, on immorality, breaking the laws of the judicial system, and a lack of productivity, then he is mistaken in that the church becomes an arm of the dominant economic system and a social apparatus for ignoring and colonizing devastated communities—for the sake of a few highly educated folks who wish to refine their manners to improve their high culture. Should that be the case, our work represents another path. We resist this view of the church and society simply because it enhances segregationalism and oppression. We have argued the opposite. Life within postmodern urban settings though revealing

75. Drucker, "Introduction: Civilizing the City," 1–8.
76. Ibid., 6.

a great deal of segmentation due to identity politics, is also seeking a unifying and localizing factor. People living in highly technocratic and global geographies are seeking to situate themselves into communities according to their many unpredicted cultural interests. In view of that, we have imagined a type of community able to allow both cultural processes, distinctiveness and commonality, so we have come out with the concept of the *mestizo/a community of mañana*. Although the *mestizo/a community of mañana* is to service all social strata and urban settings, its presence is most needed amid devastated communities which represent its immediate context.

Having said that, we find in Drucker's perception an attractive principle for community development within U.S. urban setings. That is, urban nonprofit organizations such as churches are *shaping social agents* and key factors in the process of community regeneration. We prefer the term "community regeneration" to Drucker's "civilizing process," in order to refer to that desired future that a community imagines for itself. This other side of Drucker's view is helpful, however, for churches represent a diverse and *global* community, namely, communities of the future, where "individuals in the city [are offered] an opportunity to achieve, to contribute, to matter."[77] Communities of the future, then, are "interdependent and diverse, embracing differences, releasing energy, and building cohesion" in the city. [78] In this regard, Drucker's view of the city seems organic and appealing. Taking away the social power from the government and the private sector, Drucker advances an argument in favor of nonprofit organizations as shapers of community life and social transformation. From this angle, churches can be (trans)formative communities within the city—the community of communities. Churches represent in this scenario *mañana* shapers of city life. Churches, as non-profit organizations are to function as communities of inclusion and empowerment anticipating the future by "embracing differences, releasing social energy, and building cohesion in the city." The church represents, in Drucker's imagination an urban "sphere in which they [volunteers] are in control and a sphere in which they can make a difference."[79]

77. Ibid., 5.
78. Ibid., xi.
79. Ibid., 6.

In a sense, Drucker's (positive) perception of the church supports our understanding of the Latino/a urban church as one based on commonality, interrelationality, and futurity. Next we will explore what it means to *accompany* the poor as a *Mestizo/a community of mañana* within an urban context and from the perspective of community organizing.

The Christian Community as Organizers of Mañana Life

THE EUCHARISTIC PRACTICE: ORGANIZING MAÑANA LIFE BY CREATING COMMONALITY AND SELF-AFFIRMATION

Kretzmann-McKnight taught us that communities are constructive forces in the developmental and organizational process. Drucker directed us to churches—in their nature of nonprofit organizations—as *that type* of community possessing the most leverage in shaping a city's future. How, then, is a Christian community to walk with impoverished-devastated communities, seeking a transformation?

Roberto Goizueta argues:

> Unless social transformation is rooted in an everyday *accompaniment* of the poor, that is, in the everyday act of walking with, living with, breaking bread with particular poor persons in the concreteness of the poor person's everyday struggle for survival, the transformation of social structures will, in the long run, simply perpetuate the oppression of the poor.[80]

Goizueta insinuates, as we have commented before, that the praxis of *accompaniment* is indeed a more subversive and domestic action than any historical-political praxis attempting to overthrow political or economic power structures. Goizueta's proposal of *accompaniment* points to an ecclesial praxis in the daily, in the domestic, in the cultural life of the impoverished community. In this sense, the church represents the "crossroads" of all these historical realities, a home, a family, a worship place—a place of survival and cultural dignity that allows its members to resist the ideological-economic-cultural pressures imposed by the majority culture.

The *mestizo/a community of mañana* is to *walk with* the community as a *crossroads* church, as a eucharistic church; a place where

80. Goizueta, *Caminemos con Jesús*, 207.

a person in the diverse and multifaceted community can abide along with others finding commonality and affirmation. Jesus exercised this eucharistic praxis by opening the table to the sinner and the outcast of his generation and by so doing he created a common space for the *other*, a "common Eucharistic table" where the *others* became *hermanos/as* (brothers/sisters), family.[81] A eucharistic Christopraxis necessarily points to *mestizaje*. And *mestizaje* is not, as Teresa Chavez Sauceda reminds us, the "homogenization of humanity but a unity of the human family symbolized in the table fellowship of Jesus."[82] In short, at the table of Jesus the different subjects became one *in him*. Should not this eucharistic Christopraxis be perpetuated today by the praxis of the *Mestizo/a community of mañana?*

THE PRACTICE OF PROCLAMATION: ORGANIZING MAÑANA LIFE BY INTERSECTING THE STORY OF THE TARGET COMMUNITY AND BECOMING THE LIVING EXEGESIS OF CHRIST'S NARRATIVE

In a different fashion, Bryant Myers concurs with Goizueta's view of *accompaniment* in his work *Walking with the Poor*. Myers sees the development and transformation of a given community as "the convergence of stories." There are always two stories within a community, Myers contends, "the history of the community and the story of God at work in the community."[83] The specific shape of transformation rests, according to Myers, in the way a community appropriates the "story" which will be normative for such a change. Since Myers is arguing from a Christian (evangelical) perspective, he sees that every community "and every one in it is facing a choice" against the larger story of God's salvation in human history.[84] The answer to community's questions, *what is a better future? What is well-being? What is abundant life?* will be answered based on the "normative story" the community chooses to appropriate.[85] For Myers, authentic and holistic community transformation occurs:

---

81. Eliseo Pérez Alvarez develops this theme beautifully in his Christological treatise from a Latino/a perspective. See Perez Alvarez, "In Memory of Me."

82. Chavez Sauceda, "Love in the Crossroads: Stepping-Stones to the Doctrine of God in Hispanic/Latino Theology." 30.

83. See Myers, *Walking with the Poor*, 111.

84. Ibid., 112.

85. Ibid., 113.

[W]ithin the larger story of creation, fall, redemption, and the
second coming of Christ, at which final judgment will be made
. . . Only by accepting God's salvation in Christ can people and
the community redirect the trajectory of their story, poor and
non-poor.[86]

A better future, for Myers, is kingdom-future, is shalom-future.
Shalom represents justice, peace, mutual love, inclusiveness, physi-
cal health, human purpose—in short abundant life. The role of the
Christian community is, in simple terms, to witness this kingdom story.
Thus for Myers,

It is impossible to imagine a transforming community without
a transforming church in its midst. Such a church is in love with
God and with all its neighbors, celebrating everything that is for
life and being a prophetic voice, telling the truth about everything that is against or that undermines life.[87]

The church walking with the poor as a transforming partner means for
Myers three things: One, the church must become a servant and source
of encouragement to its community; two, the church must become a
source of value-formation within the community; and three, the church
should read biblical story as "its own story" applying it to the concrete
circumstances of its time, place, and culture.[88]

Both Goizueta and Myers concur with our community organizing
perspective that sees the community as participating in its own process of transformation. Both expositors see the church as a partner of
the community-in-transformation as a source of encouragement and
Christian identity. Also, Goizueta as well as Myers view the church assuming concrete historical steps of walking with the community toward
transformation.

Although both would argue that the church must witness to Jesus,
they would differ in what they mean by witnessing to Jesus. Goizueta
is theologizing from the perspective of popular religion (Roman
Catholicism), so witnessing is, in part, constructed by popular practices and the hermeneutics of his tradition. Myers argues more from an
evangelical perspective, where biblical narrative is the formative factor

86. Ibid., 112.
87. Ibid., 115.
88. Ibid., 127–28.

for praxis. Yet, Myers acknowledges a great deal of popular construction as the community itself decides what story they deem as normative for their transformation.

Myers' view of transformation, as the "convergence of two stories," points to a dynamic model of appropriating and incarnating the biblical praxis of Jesus in history (Christopraxis). From our perspective, the Spirit of God is the historical transcendent subject able to assist the church in the act of intersecting with the community's stories. We have seen this phenomenon in many biblical instances. For example, God's historical transcendence assists: Moses in intersecting with the stories of the Hebrew people (Exodus 3–4); the prophets in intersecting with Israel's stories (e.g., Jeremiah 1—2); Jesus of Nazareth in intersecting with the stories of the Jewish people (e.g., Luke 4); the New Testament church in intersecting with the world's stories (e.g., Acts 1:8). These intersections represent, as we have argued, cultural creations of the Spirit. As Jesus, the *mestizo/a communities of mañana,* in the power of the Spirit and as a *proclamation community,* is to intersect with the stories of the target community with the transformational story of Jesus life, death, and resurrection. This calls for a life of radical hope and radical belief, that is, a *mañana way* of living the kingdom of God.

The Pastoral Practice: Organizing Mañana Life by Becoming a Healing-serving Community

The Latino/a church as a community of the Spirit—resurrected culture— or *mañana* community is a source of identity, survival, and renewal for the Latino/a people. All these items do not emerge automatically in the community but are built through church processes. Current social and religious research substantiates this perception. For instance, Andrea and Grace Dyrness, in collaboration with the James Irvine Foundation and other supporters, report their findings in their publication entitled *Faith Works: Religious Communities Building Neighborhoods.*[89] They concentrate on FAITHS Initiative programs as conducted in the areas of San Francisco and Santa Barbara County. In the summary of the publication they acknowledge the key role religious communities, such

---

89. Dyrness and Dyrness, *Faith Works.* Also an excellent research has been gathered and interpreted by Ramírez-Jonhson and Hernandez from a Hispanic-Adventist perspective. See Ramírez-Johnson and Hernandez, *Avance.*

as churches, synagogues, and mosques, play in the transformation of the community. Religious communities, they express, are:

> [U]nique contributors to community building efforts . . . they have a natural connection to the needs of the community . . . maintain connections with key stakeholders and decision-makers of public policy . . . [and] build social capital by crossing faith, class, and racial divides.[90]

In their research they focus on religious community because in reality these communities are global (transnational) communities serving society in general as "ports of entry for immigrant population, sources of human value or dignity, and inclusive environments."[91] In essence, they interpret religious communities as "neutral spaces" of social subsistence.

In Dyrness-Dyrness' perception, the role of churches in building neighborhoods is fourfold. One, churches are focal centers of social services. It is an acknowledged fact that churches "care for the disenfranchised, feed the homeless . . . bring order out of chaos and provide structure and meaning for the people."[92] Two, church leaders tend to be visionary agents advocating for social justice in their communities. They easily connect and network with community organizations and foundations to act collectively in favor of the neighborhood. In this sense, churches can offer the neighborhood a "visionary framework"[93] by which to operate as a mechanism of social action. Three, churches are "inclusivistic" communities capable of constructing a culture of meaning, social reconciliation, and social capital in the neighborhood. Dyrness-Dyrness see that: "Religious institutions can be powerful forces for change, especially when crossing faith, class, race and other divides."[94] Finally, churches are *loci* of influence in the sociopolitical arena: "Congregations often have members who are connected to public and private stakeholders that can affect policy."[95]

---

90. Dyrness and Dyrness, *Faith Works*, 5.

91. Ibid., 7. Another significant work that substantially supports this conclusion is Vásquez and Marquardt, *Globalizing the Sacred*.

92. Ibid., 11.

93. Ibid., 93.

94. Ibid.

95. Ibid., 12.

Dyrness-Dyrness have pointed, in their findings, to the pastoral praxis of the *mestizo/a community of mañana*. In Matthew 9:35–38, we find Jesus' pastoral praxis depicted as follows:

> Then Jesus went about all the cities and villages, teaching in their synagogues, and proclaiming the good news of the king-dom, and curing every disease and every sickness. When he saw the crowds, he had compassion for them, because they were harassed and helpless, like sheep without a shepherd. Then he said to his disciples, "The harvest is plentiful, but the laborers are few; therefore ask the Lord of the harvest to send out labor-ers into his harvest."

Jesus' missiological-pastoral praxis was very domestic, to use Goizueta's language. Assuming that Jesus is not historically crippled and contin-ues to walk today through his Spirit in the church, then, Jesus' praxis embraces walking in the cities with diseased/ impoverished/disenfran-chised communities in the power of the Spirit—charismatically. Jesus' praxis should become good news for such a community. Pastoral Christopraxis does not merely represent "social services" but a *new so-cial reality*. Pastoral Christopraxis also suggests the ability to see people, to discern their stories, and to empathize with them with *sentimiento*. Pastoral Christopraxis means becoming a *serving* community which is also a *healing community* in the city. So, the pastoral praxis of the *mestizo/a community of mañana* centers on social processes, visionary processes, empathizing communal processes, and pastoral processes that witness to Jesus and his continuous healing power. Christo-praxic healing goes beyond individual-physical restoration; it restores any social, cultural, psychological, theological, and political handicap and glorifies God by witnessing to Jesus' *peace*.

Conclusions

We have mentioned before that the *mestizo/a community of mañana* is to be a community of survival, hope, and belief where the future will be transformed to bringing justice, liberation, and life by the *aleteo del Espíritu*. Further, we have complied with Justo González's challenge that the church must find ways to perpetuate a social testimony in our communities—that witnesses to Jesus and unleashes community trans-formation. We have suggested that the ecclesial praxis of *community organizing* is one of these testimonies. The church, we have shown, is the key communal agent—God's transformational parlance—to bring about regeneration to community, the city, and barrio life.

Latino/a communities in the United States are by and large impoverished communities, hence the role of *mestizo/a communities of mañana* as transformative agents of the barrio and the city is more crucial than ever. *Community organizing* as an ecclesial praxis is a form of Christopraxis. The *mestizo/a community of mañana* is to organize the communal life in a *mañana way* to bring about authentic transformation. Likewise, Virgilio Elizondo also concludes that *community organizing* is an appropriate praxis with transformative attributes. He declares,

> The poor and marginalized of society can be transformed in their encounter with the risen Lord . . . those who recognize that their gift of poverty and marginalization is given to them precisely to act as the agents of liberation for their entire group—powerful and powerless alike. . . . This is exactly what is beginning to happen in various *community organizations* in some of the key American urban centers where there are heavy concentrations of Spanish-speaking peoples. . . .[96]

In an act of radical hope and belief, therefore, the *mestizo/a community of mañana* is to exercise a threefold ecclesial praxis: eucharistic praxis, proclamation praxis, and pastoral praxis, in view of accompanying impoverished Latino/a communities, into a journey of transformation. Accordantly, the Latino/a church as the *mestizo/a community of mañana* is to become an eucharistic community of inclusion and diversity, a proclamation community which reflects the intersection of the Spirit with culture, and a pastoral community that unleashes *mañana* processes within the Latino/a community by and large. These Latino/a forms of Christopraxis entail the symbiosis of the Pentecost and the cross. The Pentecost represents where the Church is in Christ, while the cross points to where the church is in the larger culture. The Pentecost means *mañana; the cross* means the power to radically question the present in its many material forms.

Conclusively then, Latino/a theology can transform Latino/a communities by becoming a critical discourse that *imagines* and *calls* the

---

96. Elizondo, *Galilean Journey*, 117, emphasis added.

Latino/a church to become a *mestizo/a community of mañana*. Such a community, for the sake of becoming a source of survival, hope, and belief for the non-confessing communities, lives *eucharistically, proclamationally, and pastorally* with the hope and the practiced-belief that the future will be transformed to bring justice, liberation, and life by the *aleteo del Espíritu*.

¡Qué será, será!
Whatever will be, will be!

Conclusion

EVERY THEOLOGY IS SOMEBODY'S STORY. LATINO/A THEOLOGY OF THE
Spirit—*the story of a verb becoming repetitiously a noun*—is the narrative of the praxis of the Spirit of Christ in the *becoming* of the church of
Jesus Christ, and so, of the church of Jesus Christ in the *becoming* of the
practice of Christ's peace. From the Book of the prophet Isaiah we read
the following words:

> Give ear and come to me;
> hear me, that your soul may live.
> I will *make an everlasting covenant* with you,
> my faithful love promised to David.
> See, *I have made him a witness to the peoples,*
> leader and commander of the peoples.
> Surely you will summon nations you know not,
> and nations that do not know you will hasten to you,
> because of the LORD your God,
> the Holy One of Israel,
> for *he has endowed you with splendor.*
> (Isa 55:3–5 NIV, emphasis added)

Through the pages of this work, we have used our Latino/a imagination
to envision a way to hear, embodied, and transmit God's *pneumaloquence*—God's "splendor."

The question that fueled the *becoming* of liberation theology—*how
to speak of God as father in an inhuman world?*—can only be answered,
we have argued, by conceiving a theology that allows God to be heard
as a father. So, it is not so much about *speaking* in the name of God but,
theologically, letting Him speak through our discourses—that is, a theology that acknowledges its own limitations, that is self-suspicious, and at
the same time that dreams, imagines, struggles for a way to *make visible*
the realities conceived in the *created* invisible realm. Doing theology,
as Gutiérrez has acknowledged, is a spiritual enterprise. By listening to
God's Spirit *a priori*, our theological *souls* (discourses) may receive *life*

and serve as *theologia a Deo docetur, Deum docet, et ad Deum ducit—a posteriori*. Through our work we have suggested that this task—the transformation of theological process itself—constitutes the beginning of a transformational discourse, requiring another cultural paradigm, namely, a *Spirit-friendly postmodern paradigm*.

By means of such a paradigm, Latino/a theologizing may see the intersection of the Spirit with culture out of which the creation of the culture of the Spirit is a consequence. This *cultural creation* of the Spirit is bound by "an everlasting covenant" with God in Jesus Christ, and thus represents the everlasting culture of the Spirit of Christ—the cultural sphere *where* revelation and praxis is to be authored by God's Spirit. Culture, we have insisted, appeals to us as the most appropriate theological category to speak of the church within a postmodern context.

That having been established, our cultural vision is contingent on the narratives of the Pentecost and the cross. The Pentecost Story informs a *Latino/a theology of the Spirit* about the complexity of Christian experience—polyphonic, diverse, heterogeneous. Such an experience is of intersubjective nature and unable to be understood on phenomenological-anthropological grounds, thus requiring the (*renvoi*) relational authoring of the Spirit, who *mediates* Jesus Christ's "big story" with our own. The narratives of the Pentecost and the cross are to be understood as a symbiotic reality communicated in human experience and cultural practices by the Spirit. Cruciformity—life according to the cross—conveys a *lifestyle* articulated in the domestic practices of everyday life. In this sense, cruciformity represents the *social ethics* of the Pentecost-shaped experience. We are to live symbiotically as a Pentecost-shaped cruciform community. Cruciformity is living *lo cotidiano* in dynamic correspondence with the Pentecost Story. Cruciformity is living life subversively and domestically in culture, embodying and transmitting—through cultural practices—the message of peace of Christ Jesus. In this way the church is perceived as God's chosen agent of transformation, the transformational parlance manifesting God's *pneumaloquence* in culture by and large—"a witness to the peoples." This, in essence, constitutes the ecclesiological cultural vision informing Latino/a theology of the Spirit.

We concluded our journey by articulating a *Latino/a theology of the Spirit*—a *verb* becoming repetitiously a *noun*—and constructing three ecclesial images that appeal, in our judgment, to the urban Latino/a cultural and religious reality. These images recapitulate, we contend, three major theological productions so far achieved by Latino/a theologizing: *mestizaje, accompaniment,* and *mañana.*

We have argued that *mestizaje* adds a *native Latino/a* categorical understanding to the issue of identity within postmodern theory, for it points to the interrelationality of our stories with God's big story.[1] That is, the Spirit reorders life at the juncture of these narratives (God and human self) and incomprehensibly creates *convivencia* (commonality) and *dignidad* (affirmation of the self) amid a noisy, emerging, and heterogeneous community.

Next, we modified the concept of *accompaniment*—developed by Goizueta—to represent the social paradigm for *situating* the self and the *church* as *mediated* by the Spirit. Although we interacted critically with Goizueta's understanding of physical sacramentality, overall we are appreciative of the concept of accompaniment. It certainly grounds Christian experience in community and cultural practices, thus representing a *mode* of cruciformity. That said, we attempted to complement *accompaniment* with the *Pentecost* component in view of a biblical and ecumenical understanding.

A third Latino/a image we incorporated in our construction was the eschatological concept of *mañana,* brought about to Latino/a theologizing by Justo González. *Mañana* is fundamentally, we maintain, a Pentecost-cruciform concept. Thus, we interacted with *mañana* theology by tailoring three domestic concepts highly functional among Latinos/as: *mañana* thought pointing to the church as a community of survival, *mañana* talk pointing to the church as a community of hope, and *mañana* walk pointing to the church as a source of daily belief-practice. This way, we nailed down the affirmation that the Latino/a church shall become the embodiment of *mañana* story; the story of the mestizo/a community of the Spirit, moving toward God's

1. Goizueta might differ from us on this perception if he *reads* our understanding through the lenses of Lyotard's postmodern description. Goizueta clearly challenges such a definition of the self for it conceives the same as 'radically heterogeneous' or as he calls it "an artificial pastiche radically disparate and ever fluctuating relations, identities . . ." Goizueta's disregards such a vision of the human self for "the self as such does not exist." Goizueta, *Caminemos con Jesús,* 137. We, on the other hand, see the self as (contextually) heterogeneous, fluctuating, seeking for self-definition without a fixed directress thus needing *more than social location* in order to find true meaning (adhesion to a complementing trajectory). Even as such, the Spirit of God *accompanies* the human unstable-psyche into communion with God, itself, and others.

promise future in today's challenging context. We concluded by offering a rather practical illustration via *community organizing* showing how the *mestizo/a community of mañana* is to function culturally and transformationally within today's impoverished communities, emphasizing the clear commitment among the poor and the weak. After underlining the unique role the Latino/a church plays amid impoverished and devastated communities, we were able to discern three transformational ecclesial practices: eucharistic presence, proclamatory presence, and pastoral presence.

These ecclesial-cultural practices *reflect*, we hope, the emergent, heterogeneous, communal, and domestic character *of* our Latino/a people. At the same time, these practices *refract* the Pentecost-cruciform character of Jesus Christ *upon* our Latino/a people. This poses to the *mestizo/*a *community* of *mañana* the mission to persuade by means of inclusive love, joyous relationality, and transformational hope Latino/a culture, by and large. In one sentence, the mission of the Latino/a church resumes in the practice of *divine peace* amidst the violent context making up the cultural domains that make up Latino/a life. In such a case the most important mission of the Latino/a church is to bring about *mañana culture*. For the almighty Lord of peace has endowed his church with persuasive "splendor."

Future Commutings

The *Mestizo/a Community of Mañana* means for us a *commuting* and a *communal* experience. In the production of these three ecclesial images, we are indebted to the Latino/a people (our cultural home), to the diverse Latino/a church (Catholic, Protestant, and else—our place of renewal), and to the Latino/a and non-Latino/a theology (the mirror of our imagination).

Evidently, we are not the author of these ecclesial images; a Latino/a theologian of the Spirit, just like storm chasers, narrates and tells about the happenings at the juncture of Christ's Spirit and Latino/a culture. By so doing, Latino/a theologians of the Spirit are to assist the Latino/a church to conform to the truthfulness of its polyphonic and cruciform cultural condition, within American culture, *as envisioned by God*. Also, Latino/a theologians of the Spirit are to *walk with* Latino/a communities co-imagining and co-constructing cultural practices that can witness to

Jesus Christ as *divine presence of peace*: as inclusive environments, as communal wombs of identity, and as empowering systemic matrices of the Spirit of *mañana*.

We claim no completion of our task here. A *Latino/a Theology of the Spirit* is and must remain a pilgrimage with several sojourns— a verb *becoming* a noun. Our work points to Latino/a theology in-the-making, never a complete endeavor, and welcomes criticism and reconstructions.

Second, our *Spirit-friendly* postmodern paradigm is a seed (a light at the end of the tunnel) needing development and critique. Seasoned and creative theologians will find it a part of a whole.

Third, the understanding of the Spirit of Christ as the *compañero/a del alma* (soul companion) in a postmodern sense must be followed up. We see it as a fertile field. Perhaps the recent works of Leonardo Boff, the Eastern Orthodox theologian David Hart, and the Latino theologian Alex García-Rivera, to name some, could continue to help us advance this discussion if we can pair with their outstanding knowledge of the Classics, mysticism, and philosophical fluency.

Fourth, we have offered a valid and relevant social practice (community organizing), what we failed in accomplishing was to accompany it by a case study—a task we originally envisioned but were unable to achieve due to the scope of this work. This could become a future project.

Last but not least, given the fact that the author holds multiple spiritualities (Catholic Benedictine, Reformed-Baptist, Charismatic), a future theological urgency is in the line of the emerging field of *pneumatology of religion*, where we could explore the juncture of the Spirit and popular religiosity among Roman Catholicism and Pentecostal spiritualities.

Bibliography

Allison, Brian, and Phil Race. *The Student's Guide to Preparing Dissertations and Theses.* 2nd ed. New York: RoutledgeFalmer, 2004.

Anderson, Ray S. *Historical Transcendence and the Reality of God: A Christological Critique.* London: G. Chapman, 1975.

———. *On Being Human: Essays in Theological Anthropology.* Pasadena: Fuller Seminary Press, 1991. First published 1982 by Eerdmans.

———. *Ministry on the Fireline: A Practical Theology for an Empowered Church.* Downers Grove, IL: IntgerVarsity, 1993.

———. *The Shape of Practical Theology: Empowering Ministry with Theological Praxis.* Downers Grove, IL: InterVarsity, 2001.

Aquino, María Pilar. "Directions and Foundations of Hispanic/Latino Theology: Toward a *Mestiza* Theology of Liberation." *Journal of Hispanic/Latino Theology* 1, no. 1 (1993): 5–21.

———. "Theological Method in U.S. Latino/a Theology: Toward an Intercultural Theology for the Third Millennium." In *From the Heart of Our People: Latino/a Explorations in Catholic Systematic Theology,* edited by Orlando O. Espín and Miguel H. Díaz, 6–48. Maryknoll, NY: Orbis, 1999.

Aquino, María Pilar, Daisy L. Machado, and Jeanette Rodríguez, eds. *A Reader in Latina Feminist Theology: Religion and Justice.* Austin: University of Texas Press, 2002.

Barth, Karl. *Church Dogmatics, Vol. III, Part 2.* Edinburgh: T & T Clark, 1960.

———. *Church Dogmatics, Vol. IV, Part 1.* Edinburgh: T & T Clark, 1969.

———. "Concluding Unscientific Postscript on Schleiermacher." In *The Theology of Schleiermacher,* 261–79. Grand Rapids, MI: Eerdmans, 1982.

———. *The Humanity of God.* Richmond: John Knox, 1960.

———. "The Place of Theology." In *Theological Foundations for Ministry,* edited by Ray S. Anderson, 22–58. Grand Rapids, MI: Edermans, 1979.

Bertrán, Gonzalo Aguirre. *El Proceso de Aculturación.* Mexico City: Universidad Iberoamericana, 1970 [1958].

Bevans, Stephen B. *Models of Contextual Theologies.* Rev. ed. Faith and Culture Series. Maryknoll: Orbis, 1992.

Boff, Leonardo. *Jesucristo el Libertador: Ensayo de Cristología Crítica para Nuestro Tiempo.* Translated by María E. Rodríguez. Buenos Aires: Latinoamerica Libros S.R.L., 1974.

———. *Textos Selectos.* Translated by Justiniano Beltran. Santa Fe de Bogota: Ediciones Paulinas, 1992.

———. *Gracia y Experiencia Humana.* Madrid: Editorial Trotta, 2001.

———. *La Crísis como Oportunidad de Crecimiento: Vida Según el Espíritu.* Santander: Sal Terrae, 2004.

Bonhoeffer, Dietrich. *The Cost of Discipleship*. New York: Collier, 1963.

_____. *Sanctorum Communio: A Dogmatic Inquiry into the Sociology of the Church*. London: Collins, 1963.

Brown, Raymond E. *An Introduction to the New Testament*. New York: Doubleday, 1997.

Browning, Don S. *A Fundamental Practical Theology: Descriptive and Strategic Proposals*. Minneapolis: Fortress, 1996.

Bruce, F. F. *The Acts of the Apostles: The Greek Text with Introduction and Commentary*. Grand Rapids, MI: Eerdmans, 1986. First published 1951 by Tyndale.

──────. *Paul: Apostle of the Heart Set Free*. Grand Rapids, MI: Eerdmans, 2000. First published 1977 by Paternoster.

Burnett, Richard E. *Karl Barth's Theological Exegesis: The Hermeneutical Principles of the Romerbrief Period*. Grand Rapids, MI: Eerdmans, 2004.

Cadena, R. Gilbert. "The Social Location of Liberation Theology: From Latin America to the United States." In *Hispanic/Latino Theology: Challenge and Promise*, edited by Ada María Isasi-Díaz and Fernando F. Segovia, 167–82. Minneapolis: Fortress, 1996.

Cassese, Giacomo. "De la Iglesia y el Estado Omnipotente: ¿Cómo Debemos Vivir la Fe en el Imperio?" *Apuntes* 20, no. 3 (2000): 104–117.

Chavez Sauceda, Teresa. "Love in the Crossroads: Stepping-Stones to the Doctrine of God in the Hispanic/Latino Theology." In *Teologia en Conjunto: A Collaborative Hispanic Protestant Theology*, edited Jose David Rodriquez and Loida I. Martell-Otero, 22–32. Louisiana: Westminster John Knox, 1997.

Conde-Frazier, Elizabeth. *Hispanic Bible Institutes: A Community of Theological Construction*. Scranton, PA: University of Scranton Press, 2004.

──────. "Hispanic Protestant Spirituality." In *Teología en Conjunto: A Collaborative Hispanic Protestant Theology*, edited José David Rodríguez and Loida I. Martell-Otero, 125–45. Lousville: Westminster John Knox, 1997.

Congar, Yves. *The Word and the Spirit*. San Francisco: Harper & Row, 1986.

Costas, Orlando E. *Christ Outside the Gate: Mission Beyond Christendom*. Maryknoll, NY: Orbis, 1993.

──────. *Liberating News: A Theology of Contextual Evangelization*. Grand Rapids: Eerdmans, 1989.

de Caussade, Jean-Pierre. *The Sacrament of the Present Moment*. Translated by Kitty Muggeridge. San Francisco: HarperSanFrancisco, 1989. First published 1982 by Harper & Row.

de Certeau, Michel. *The Practice of Everyday Life*. Translated by Steven Rendall. Los Angeles: University of California Press, 1984.

De La Torre, Miguel A., and Edwin David Aponte. *Introducing Latino/a Theologies*. Maryknoll, New York: Orbis, 2001.

De La Torre, Miguel A., and Gastón Espinosa, eds. *Rethinking Latino(a) Religion and Identity*. Cleveland: Pilgrim, 2006.

Debray, Régis. *Transmitting Culture*. Translated by Eric Rauth. European Perspectives. New York: Columbia University Press, 2000.

Deck, Allan Figueroa. *The Second Wave: Hispanic Ministry and the Evangelization of Cultures*. New York: Paulist, 1989.

————, editor. *Frontiers of Hispanic Theology in the United States*. Maryknoll: Orbis, 1992.

Delgado, Richard, and Jean Stefancic, eds. *The Latino/a Condition*. New York: New York University Press, 1998.

Derrida, Jacques. "Structure, Sign, and Play in the Discurse of Human Sciences." In *Critical Theory since Plato*, edited by Hazard Adas. New York: Harcourt Brace Jovanonich, 1992.

Drucker, Peter F. "Introduction: Civilizing the City." In *The Community of the Future*, edited by Frances Hesselbein, Marshall Goldsmith, Richard Beckhard, and Richard Schubert, 1–8. Drucker Foundation Future Series. San Francisco: Jossey-Bass, 1998.

————. "Introduction: Toward the New Organization." In *The Organization of the Future*, edited by Frances Hesselbein, Marshall Goldsmith, and Richard Beckhard, 1–8. Drucker Foundation Future Series. San Francisco: Jossey-Bass, 1997.

Dunn, James D. G. *The Theology of Paul the Apostle*. Grand Rapids, MI: Eerdmanns, 1998.

————. *Christianity in the Making: Jesus Remembered*. 2 vols. Grand Rapids, MI: Eerdmans, 2003.

Dyrness, Grace Roberts, and Andrea E.Dyrness. *Faith Works: Religious Communities Building Neighborhoods*. Los Angeles: Center for Religion and Civic Culture, University of Southern California, 2002.

Dyrness, William A. *The Earth Is God's: A Theology of North American Culture*. Faith and Cultures. Maryknoll, NY: Orbis, 1997.

Elizondo, Virgil. *Guadalupe: Mother of the New Creation*. Maryknoll, NY: Orbis, 1997.

————. *The Future is Mestizo: Life Where Cultures Meet*. New York: Crossroad, 1988.

Elizondo, Virgilio P. *Galilean Journey: The Mexican Promise*. Maryknoll, NY: Orbis, 1983.

Escobar, Samuel. *Changing Tides: Latin America & World Mission Today*. Maryknoll, NY: Orbis, 2002.

Espín, Orlando O. "Grace and Humanness: A Latino/a Perspective." In *We Are a People! Initiatives in Hispanic American Theology*, edited by Roberto S. Goizueta, 133–64. Minneapolis: Fortress, 1992.

Espín, Orlando O., and Miguel H. Díaz, eds. *From the Heart of Our People: Latino/a Explorations in Catholic Systematic Theology*. Maryknoll, NY: Orbis, 1999.

Espinoza, L. G. "Latino/a Identity and Multi-Identity." In *The Latino/a Condition: A Critical Reader*, edited by Richard Delgado and Jean Stefancic, 17–23. New York: New York University Press, 1998.

Falicov, Celia Jaes. *Latino Families in Therapy: A Guide to Multicultural Practice*. New York: Guilford, 1998.

Farrer, Austin. *Reflective Faith*. Grand Rapids, MI: Eerdmans, 1974.

————. *Faith and Speculation: An Essay in Philosophical Theology*. Edinburgh: T & T Clark, 1988.

Fernández, Eduardo. *La Cosecha: Harvesting United States Hispanic Theology (1972–1978)*. Collegeville, MN: Liturgical, 2000.

Floristán, Casiano. "Naturaleza de la Teología Práctica." *Journal of Hispanic/Latino Theology* 6, no. 2 (1998): 5–17.

———. *Teología Práctica: Teoría y Praxis de laón Pastoral*. 3rd ed. Salamanca: Ediciones Sigueme, 1998.

Frank, Erich. *Philosophical Understanding and Religious Truth*. New York: Oxford University Press, 1966.

Friesen, Duane K. *Artists, Citizens, Philosophers: Seeking the Peace of the Ciy, an Anabaptist Theology of Culture*. Scottdale, PA: Herald, 2000.

García, Ismael. *Dignidad: Ethics through Hispanic Eyes*. Nashvilee: Abingdon, 1997.

García, Sixto J. "Sources and Loci of Hispanic Theology." *Journal of Hispanic/Latino Theology* 1, no. 1 (1993): 22–43.

García-Johnson, Oscar. "Acentos Eticos de John H. Yoder y Alternativas Eticas Latinas en E.E.U.U." Lecture on Theological Ethics for the Fraternidad Teológica Latinoamericana, Los Angeles Chapter, Pasadena, CA, April 21, 2004.

García-Rivera, Alex. "Creator of the Visible and the Invisible: Liberation Theology, Postmodernism, and the Spiritual." *Journal of Hispanic/Latino Theology* 3, no. 4 (1996): 35–56.

———. *The Community of the Beautiful: A Theological Aesthetics*. Collegeville, Minn.: Liturgical, 1999.

Gelpi, Don. *The Turn to Experience in Contemporary Theology*. New York: Paulist, 1994.

Girard, Rene. *Violence and the Sacred*. Translated by Patrick Gregory. Baltimore: The John Hopkins University Press, 1992.

Goizueta, Roberto S. "Liberation and Method: The Dialectical Method of Enrique Dussel." In *Pedagogy of God's Image: Essays on Symbol and the Religious Imagination*, edited by Robert Masson, 113–134. Chico, CA: Scholars, 1982.

———. "U.S. Hispanic Mestizaje and Theological Method." In *Migrants and Refugees*, edited by Dietmar Mieth and Lisa Sowle Cahill, 22–30. London: SCM, 1993.

———. *Caminemos con Jesús: Toward a Hispanic/Latino Theology of Accompaniment*. Maryknoll, NY: Orbis, 1995.

González, Justo L. *Mañana: Christian Theology from a Hispanic Perspective*. Nashville: Abingdon Press, 1990.

———. *Out of Every Tribe and Nation: Christian Theology at the Ethnic Roundtable*. Nashville: Abingdon, 1992.

———. "Metamodern Aliens in Postmodern Jerusalem." In *Hispanic/Latino Theology: Challenge and Promise*, edited by Ada María Isasi-Díaz and Fernando F. Segovia, 340–50. Minneapolis: Fortress, 1996.

———. *Santa Biblia: The Bible through Hispanic Eyes*. Nashville: Abingdon, 1996.

———. *Acts: The Gospel of the Spirit*. Maryknoll, NY: Orbis, 2001.

Gorman, Michael J. *Cruciformity: Paul's Narrative Spirituality of the Cross*. Grand Rapids, MI: Eerdmans, 2001.

Graham, Elaine. "Pastoral Theology." In *The Oxford Companion to Christian Thought*, edited by Adrian Hastings, Alistair Mason and Hugh Pyper, 519–20. New York: Oxford University Press, 2000.

Greene, Colin J. D. *Christology in Cultural Perspective: Marking out the Horizons*. Grand Rapids, MI: Eerdmans, 2003.

Grenz, Stanley. *A Primer on Postmodernism*. Grand Rapids, MI: Eerdmans, 1996.

Gruzinski, Serge. *The Mestizo Mind: The Intellectual Dynamics of Colonization and Globalization*. Translated by Deke Dusinberre. New York: Routledge Taylor & Francis, 2002.

Gutiérrez, Gustavo. *Teología de la Liberación: Perspectivas*. 16th ed. Salamanca: Sigueme, 1999.

———. "Labor y Contenido de la Teología de la Liberación." In *La Teología de la Liberación*, ed. Christopher Rowland, 41–63. Madrid: Cambridge University Press, 2000.

Hancock, Curtis L., and Brendan Sweetman, eds. *Faith & the Life of the Intellect*. Washington, D.C.: The Catholic University of America Press, 2003.

Hart, David Bentley. *The Beauty of the Infinity: The Aesthetics of the Christian Truth*. Grand Rapids, MI: Eerdmans, 2003.

Hauerwas, Stanley, Chris K. Huebner, Harry J. Huebner, and Mark Thiessen Nation, eds. *The Wisdom of the Cross: Essays in Honor of John Howard Yoder*. Eugene, OR: Wipf & Stock, 2005. First published 1999 by Eerdmans.

Hays, Richard B. *The Moral Vision of the New Testament: Community, Cross, New Creation*. San Francisco: HarperSanFrancisco, 1996.

Heitink, Gerben. *Practical Theology: History, Theory, Action Domains*. Translated by Reinder Bruinsma. Studies in Practical Theology, edited by D. S. Browning, J. W. Fowler, F. Schweitzer, and Johannes van der Ven. Grand Rapids, MI: Eerdmans, 1999.

Herbert, Christopher. *Culture and Anomie: Ethnographic Imagination in the Nineteenth Century*. Chicago: University of Chicago Press, 1991.

Hesselbenein, Frances, Marshall Goldsmith, and Richard Beckhard, eds. *The Organization of the Future*. Drucker Foundation Future Series. San Francisco: Jossey-Bass, 1997.

Hesselbenein, Frances, Marshall Goldsmith, Richard Beckhard, and Richard Schubert, eds. *The Community of the Future*. San Francisco: Jossey-Bass, 1998.

Hunsinger, George. *Disruptive Grace: Studies in the Theology of Karl Barth*. Grand Rapids, MI: Eerdmans, 2000.

Hunt, A. M. *The Unity of the New Testament*. London: SCM, 1943.

Isasi-Díaz, Ada María. *En La Lucha/in the Struggle: Elaborating a Mujerista Theology*. Minneapolis: Fortress, 1993.

Isasi-Díaz, Ada María, and Fernando F. Segovia. *Hispanic/Latino Theology: Challenge and Promise*. Minneapolis: Fortress, 1996.

Kärkkäinen, Veli-Matti. *Pneumatology: The Holy Spirit in Ecumenical, International, and Contextual Perspective*. Grand Rapids, MI: Baker Academic, 2002.

Käsemann, Ernst. "The Saving Significance of the Death of Jesus in Paul." In *Perspectives on Paul*, translated by Margaret Kohl. Philadelphia: Fortress, 1971; reprint, Mifflingtown, Pa.: Sigler, 1996.

Kittel, Gerhard, and Gerhard Friedrich, eds. *Theological Dictionary of the New Testament*. Translated by Geoffrey William Bromiley. 10 vols. Grand Rapids, MI: Eerdmans, 1964–76.

Kretzmann, John P., and John L. Mcknight. *Building Communities from the Inside Out: A Path toward Finding and Mobilizing a Community's Assets*. Chicago, IL: ACTA, 1993.

Kroker, Arthur, Marilouise Kroker, and David Cook. "Panic Alphabet." in *Panic Encyclopedia: The Definitive Guide to the Postmodern Scene*. Montreal: New World Perspectives, 1989.

Krueger, Allan B., and Jonathan M. Orszag. "Hispanics and the Current Economic Downturn: Will the Receding Tide Sink Hispanics?" Pew Hispanic Center, January 24, 2002. http://pewhispanic.org/reports/report.php?ReportID=3 (accessed March 18, 2008).

Lawlor, Leonard. *Imagination and Chance: The Difference between the Thought of Ricoeur and Derrida*. New York: State University of New York Press, 1992.

Litonjua, M. D. "Pentecostalism in Latin America: Scrutinizing the Sign of the Times." *Journal of Hispanic/Latino Theology* 7, no. 4 (2000): 26–49.

Loder, James E. *The Logic of the Spirit: Human Development in Theological Perspective*. San Francisco: Jossey-Bass, 1998.

Lonergan, Bernard. *Method in Theology*. 2nd ed. Toronto: University of Toronto Press, 1999. First published 1972 by Herder and Herder.

"Los Tigres Del Norte: La Reina Del Sur." Fonovisa. http://www.fonovisa.com/ noticias65.html (accessed November 23, 2004; page now discontinued).

Lyotard, Jean-François. *The Postmodern Condition: A Report on Knowledge*. Translated by Geoff Bennington and Brian Massumi. Manchester: Manchester University Press, 1984.

Maddox, Randy L. "The Recovery of Theology as a Practical Discipline." *Theological Studies* 51, no. 4 (1990): 650–72.

Maldonado, David, Jr. "Doing Theology and the Anthropological Questions." In *Teología en Conjunto: A Collaborative Hispanic Protestant Theology*, edited by Jose David Rodríguez and Loida Martell-Otero, 98–111. Louisville: Wenstmister John Knox, 1997.

Martin, Ralph P. *New Testament Foundations: A Guide For Christian Students*. Vol. 2, *The Acts, The Letters, The Apocalypse*. Rev. ed. Grand Rapids, MI: Eerdmans, 1986.

Mason, T. W. "The New Testament Basis of the Doctrine of the Church." *Journal of Ecclesiastical History* 1 (1950): 1–11.

Masuzawa, Tomoko. "Culture." In *Critical Terms for Religious Studies*, edited by Mark C. Taylor, 70–93. Chicago: Chicago University Press, 1998.

Mendieta, Eduardo. "From Christendom to Polycentric Oikoumené: Modernity, Postmodernity, and Liberation Theology." *Journal of Hispanic/Latino Theology* 3, no. 4 (1996): 57–76.

Migueléz, X. *La Teología de la Liberación y su Método*. Barcelona: Herder, 1976.

Mirandé, Alfredo. *The Chicano Experience: An Alternative Perspective*. South Bend, IN: University of Notre Dame Press, 1985.

Moltmann, Jürgen. *The Church in the Power of the Spirit*. Minneapolis: Fortress, 1993.

Mühlen, Heribert. *Una Mystica Persona: Die Kirche als das Mysterium der Heilsgeschichtlichen Identität des heiligen Geistes in Christus und den Christen: Eine Person in Vielen Personen*. 3rd ed. Munich: Ferdinand Schöningh, 1968.

Muller, Richard A. *Dictionary of Latin and Greek Theological Terms: Drawn Principally from Protestant Scholastic Theology*. Grand Rapids, MI: Baker, 1993.

Murphy, Nancey C. *Reasoning and Rhetoric in Religion.* Eugene, OR: Wipf and Stock, 2001. First published 1994 by Trinity.

———. "John Howard Yoder's Systematic Defence of Christian Pacificism." In *The Wisdom of the Cross: Essays in Honor of John Howard Yoder,* edited by Stanley Hauerwas, Chris K. Huebner, Harry J. Huebner, and Mark Thiessen Nation, 45–68. Eugene, OR: Wipf & Stock, 2005. First published 1999 by Eerdmans.

Murphy, Nancey C., and George F. R. Ellis. *On the Moral Nature of the Universe: Theology, Cosmology, and Ethics.* Minneapolis: Fortress, 1996.

Myers, Bryant. *Walking with the Poor: Principles and Practices of Transformational Development.* Maryknoll, NY: Orbis, 1999.

Nation, Mark Thiessen. "John H. Yoder, Ecumenical, Neo-Anabaptist: A Bibliographical Sketch." In *The Wisdom of the Cross: Essays in Honor of John Howard Yoder,* edited by Stanley Hauerwas, Chris K. Huebner, Harry J. Huebner, and Mark Thiessen Nation, 1–23. Eugene, OR: Wipf & Stock, 2005. First published 1999 by Eerdmans.

Pedraja, Luis G. *Teología: An Introduction to Hispanic Theology.* Nashville: Abingdon, 2003.

Perez Alvarez, Eliseo. "In Memory of Me: Hispanic/Latino Christology beyond Borders." In *Teología en Conjunto: A Collaborative Hispanic Protestant Theology,* edited by Jose David Rodríguez and Loida Martell-Otero, 33–49. Louisville: Westminster John Knox, 1997.

Rahner, Karl. *Experience of the Spirit: Source of Theology.* Theological Investigations 16. New York: Crossroad, 1981.

Ramírez-Johnson, Johnny, and Edwin I. Hernández. *Avance: A Vision for a New Mañana.* Loma Linda, CA: Loma Linda University Press, 2003.

Recinos, Harold J. *Good News from the Barrio: Prophetic Witness for the Church.* Louisville: Westminster John Knox, 2006.

———. "The Barrio as the Locus of a New Church." In *Hispanic/Latino Theology: Challenge and Promise,* ed. Ada María Isasi-Díaz and Fernando F. Segovia, 183–94. Minneapolis: Fortress, 1996.

Rienecker, Fritz, and Cleon Rogers. *Linguistic Key to the Greek New Testament.* Grand Rapids, MI: Zondervan, 1980.

Rodríguez, Jeanette. "U.S. Latina/o Theology: Context and Challenge." *Journal of Hispanic/Latino Theology* 5, no. 3 (1998).

Rodríguez, José David. "On Doing Hispanic Theology." In *Teología en Conjunto: A Collaborative Hispanic Protestant Theology,* edited by José David Rodríguez and Loida Martell-Otero, 11–21. Louisville: Westminster John Knox, 1997.

Rodríguez, José David, and Loida Martell-Otero, eds. *Teología en Conjunto: A Collaborative Hispanic Protestant Theology.* Louisville: Westminster John Knox, 1997.

Rowland, Christopher, ed. *La Teología de la Liberación.* Religiones y Mitos, edited by Francisco Díaz de Velasco. Madrid: Cambridge University Press, 2000.

Sachs, John. "'Do Not Stifle the Spirit': Karl Rahner, the Legacy of Vatican II, and Its Urgency for Theology Today." *Catholic Theological Society. Proceedings* 51. (1996):17–18.

Schreiter, Robert J. "Contextualization in U.S. Hispanic Theology." *Journal of Hispanic/ Latino Theology* 8, no. 2 (2000): 18–32.

Segovia, Fernando F. "In the World but Not of It: Exile as Locus for Theology of the Diaspora." In *Hispanic/Latino Theology: Challenge and Promise*, edited by Ada María Isasi-Díaz and Fernando F. Segovia, 195–217. Minneapolis: Fortress, 1996.

"Shavu'ot." In *The Oxford Dictionary of the Jewish Religion*, edited by R. J. Zwi Werblowsky and Geoffrey Wigoder, 628–29. New York: Oxford University Press, 1997.

Sherrard, Philip. *The Eclipse of Man and Nature: An Enquiry into the Origins and Consequences of Modern Science*. West Stockbridge, MA: Lindisfarne, 1986.

Solivan, Samuel. "The Holy Spirit: A Pentecostal Hispanic Perspective." In *Teologia En Conjunto: A Collaborative Hispanic Protestant Theology*, edited by Jose David Rodríguez and Loida Martell-Otero, 50–65. Lousville: Westminster Knox, 1997.

———. *The Spirit, Pathos and Liberation: Toward an Hispanic Pentecostal Theology*. Journal of Pentecostal Theology, Supplemental Series 14. Sheffield: Sheffield Academic, 1998.

Spinoza, Benedict de. *Ethics*. The Hafner Library Classics. New York: Hafner, 1949.

Stassen, Glen Harold, Diane M. Yeager, John Howard Yoder, and H. Richard Niebuhr. *Authentic Transformation: A New Vision of Christ and Culture*. Nashville: Abingdon, 1996.

Tamayo, Juan José. "In Memoriam." *Vida y Pensamirnto* 26, no. 2 (Octubre 2006): 151–56.

Tanner, Kathryn. *Theories of Culture: A New Agenda for Theology*. Guides to Theological Inquiry, edited by Paul Lakeland and Kathryn Tanner. Minneapolis: Fortress, 1997.

Vásquez, Manuel A. "Rethinking Mestizaje." In *Rethinking Latino(a) Religion and Identity*, edited by Miguel De La Torre and Gastón Espinoza, 129-157. Cleveland: Pilgrim, 2006.

Vásquez, Manuel A., and Marie F. Marquardt. *Globalizing the Sacred: Religion Across the Americas*. New Brunswick, N.J.: Rutgers University Press, 2003.

Van Den Hengel, John. "Paul Ricoeur's Oneself as Another and Practical Theology." *Theological Studies* 55, no. 3 (1994): 458.

Villafañe, Eldin. *The Liberating Spirit: Toward a Hispanic American Pentecostal Social Ethics*. New York: University Press of America, 1992.

Villamán, Marcos J. "Church and Inculturation: Modernity and Culture in Latin America." *Journal of Hispanic/Latino Theology* 1, no. 3 (1994): 5–46.

Wathtel, Paul. *The Poverty of Affluence: A Psychological Portrait of the American Way of Life*. New York: Free Press, 1983.

Weil, Simon. *Gravity and Grace*. New York: Routledge, 1997.

William, Raymond. *Culture and Society, 1780-1950*. New York: Columbia University Press, 1983.

Wright, Robert E. "If It's Official, It Can't Be Popular? Reflections on Popular and Folk Religion." *Journal of Hispanic/Latino Theology* 1, no. 3 (1994): 47–67.

Yoder, John Howard. *The Priestly Kingdom: Social Ethics as Gospel*. South Bend, IN: University of Notre Dame Press, 1984.

———. "Armaments and Eschatology." *Studies in Christian Ethics* 1 (1988): 43–61.

———. *The Politics of Jesus: Vicit Agnus Noster*. 2nd ed. Grand Rapids, MI: Eerdmans, 1994.

Lightning Source UK Ltd.
Milton Keynes UK
UKOW01f1116150817

307336UK00002B/298/P

9 781556 357190